Scott Jehl

RESPONSIBLE
RESPONSIVE DESIGN

Publisher: Jeffrey Zeldman
Designer: Jason Santa Maria
Managing Director: Katel LeDû
Editor: Tina Lee
Technical Editor: Ethan Marcotte
Copyeditors: Caren Litherland, Rachel Kaufman
Proofreader: Caren Litherland
Compositor: Rob Weychert
Ebook Production: India Amos

ISBN: 978-1-9375571-6-4

A Book Apart
New York, New York
http://abookapart.com

10 9 8 7 6 5 4 3 2 1

TABLE OF CONTENTS

FOREWORD

THE WEB IS A SUCKER for a good metaphor. In its early days, it was our printing press; as it got older, it was our playground, then our marketplace; now, it's our photo albums, our diaries, our travelogues, our shared moments and videos and GIFs and... and, and, and. What's more, thanks to the explosive popularity of handheld, web-ready devices, the web is accessed more broadly today than at any point in its short lifespan. I think it's fair to say the web is more than the sum of its underpinnings, evolving from a tangle of wires flinging packets over HTTP to a place where we publish, we sell, we connect, we work, and we play.

But here's the thing: the web is far more fragile than we might like to admit. It's fraught with uncertainty—a connection could be dropped, or a network's latency could be too high—which means entire elements of our designs might never reach our users. Of course, it's tempting to see this as a temporary problem, one that'll gradually resolve itself as devices get better, or as networks get stronger. But between the aging infrastructure of developed economies and the popularity of cheaper, low-powered mobile devices in younger, emerging markets, it feels like we're watching a new normal emerge for the web—a medium that's accessed across the planet, but is also much, much slower than we previously thought.

This might sound scary. But that's not how this story ends.

When "mobile" first happened, we were given an opportunity: instead of defaulting to device-specific sites, we realized we could use flexible layouts and media queries to make responsive designs, layouts that could adapt to a nearly infinite array of differently sized screens.

So now, too, we have another opportunity: to ensure our layouts aren't just responsive, but sustainable—fit to deliver compelling content and rich interfaces not only to the latest devices or the widest networks, but to every glowing screen, everywhere.

Thankfully, Scott Jehl is here to show us the way.

I've had the pleasure of working with Scott on a number of responsive redesigns, and I've never encountered a designer who possesses such a keen awareness of—and respect for—the web's fragility. And in this little book, Scott will share that expertise with you, dear reader, teaching you how to build nimble, lightweight interfaces that are ready for the web's volatility.

In the past few years of designing responsively, we've been learning to let go of our need to control the width and height of our layouts. Now, Scott Jehl shows us the next step: to build responsive designs in a responsible way, to ensure they're ready not just for differently sized screens, but for the changing shape of a universal, device-agnostic web.

Let's go.

—Ethan Marcotte

INTRODUCTION

IN EARLY 2012, my wife and I rented an apartment in Siem Reap, Cambodia. She was volunteering at a children's hospital; I was clocking in remotely to build websites with my Filament Group colleagues back in the United States. I worked this way for months as we traveled the region, passing through some of the most resource-strapped places in the developing world— Laos, Indonesia, Sri Lanka, and Nepal. Each stop offered an opportunity to use the web under the same, often constrained conditions that people who live there do. It tested my assumptions as a designer and my patience as a user.

You've likely read that mobile services are the primary means of internet access for many in developing parts of the world, and my casual observations confirmed that. Glass cases displaying mobile devices I'd never seen before filled street market stalls (and helped stock my backpack with test devices). But while seemingly everyone had an internet-capable phone, I was surprised at how frequently people used cell networks to connect other devices to the web. A prepaid SIM card and a USB dongle was the usual means to get a laptop online. So it was for me too.

Using the web this way was an exercise in patience. I wasted hours toggling between partially loaded browser tabs and hitting refresh to watch another web app's loading message spin atop a blank white page, eating away at the limited data I was allotted within my prepaid SIM card. As an advocate of best practices like progressive enhancement and responsive design, I would sometimes indulge in the thought that if only these sites had been built the "right way," these problems wouldn't exist. But if I was honest, I'd concede that many such best practices weren't working as well as they could. Sadly, it appeared that the basic promise of access on the web is one we have yet to fulfill.

I'm not the first to notice. A 2014 *Wired* article described several Facebook executives' experience using their own service during a visit to Nigeria, where over 30% of internet users are on Facebook (http://bkaprt.com/rrd/0-01/):

We fired it up, and we wait... and we wait... It took a really long time. Even simple things like uploading a photo—things most Facebook users do—just weren't working. That was a pretty harsh experience for us. We'd been building an app for users like us. But we were the exception, not the rule.

We web developers tend to be an exceptional bunch. Our work demands fast, reliable networks to stream enormous amounts of data, and we have access to the latest, most capable devices. But while many of us work in relatively ideal conditions, we can't just build for users like us; we can't forget that for most of the world, the web doesn't function like this.

You may think, "But that's not my audience." And you may be right, but consider that more of the world's web traffic this year will come from cheaper, under-featured devices in emerging markets (http://bkaprt.com/rrd/0-02/). Even in some of the most developed regions, mobile connections are often slow, intermittent, and unreliable, as data plans become more expensive and limited. A quick Twitter search confirms that London's notoriously bad cell service persists, and heck, I rarely get better than an ancient EDGE connection where I live in Florida—*EDGE!*

Accessing the web reliably and efficiently isn't a given for many of our neighbors, our users, our customers. As web designers, we're well poised to improve this situation. I mention *customers* to emphasize that pushing for better access is not only an appeal for empathy, but also an opportunity to expand the reach of our services, making them more resilient for everyone.

This book is about accessibility: broadening access to the services we make without compromising features that push the web ahead. Diversity is a defining feature of the web, not a bug. We should strive to make our content and services accessible to all capable devices. If that sounds hard, well, sometimes it is. I intend to convince you that it's possible, and that it's worth it.

Let's debrief on what our users are up to, shall we?

Our diversifying web

The proof is in the numbers. In 2011, Apple sold more iOS devices than all of the computers it sold in twenty-eight years

FIG 0.1: A sampling of the variety of screen sizes we now need to support.

(http://bkaprt.com/rrd/0-03/). In 2013, global mobile data usage grew by 81% (http://bkaprt.com/rrd/0-04/). As of January 2014, 58% of Americans owned a smartphone and 42% owned a tablet, four years after the iPad's release (http://bkaprt.com/rrd/0-05/). The speed of such growth is astonishing, but it's not just mobile.

Our devices represent a broadening spectrum of form factors, feature support, environmental constraints, and uses (**FIG 0.1**). The variance in screen size alone is staggering—consider this graphic overlaying the screen dimensions of the twenty most-used devices in early 2013 (**FIG 0.2**).

Screen dimensions say nothing about a display's resolution, which may be higher than standard definition; nor do they predict a browser's viewport size, which often differs from the screen's. As designer Cennydd Bowles says, when you consider the near-infinite variability of browser viewports, the sizes we need to care about are even broader in range than screen dimension rankings might suggest (**FIG 0.3**).

Now that's fragmentation! Luckily, the problem of delivering a design that adapts fluidly across various viewport sizes has been more or less solved.

Responsive design: a responsible starting point

"This is our way forward. Rather than tailoring disconnected designs to each of an ever-increasing number of web devices, we can treat them as facets of the same experience."
—**ETHAN MARCOTTE**, "Responsive Web Design," *A List Apart*

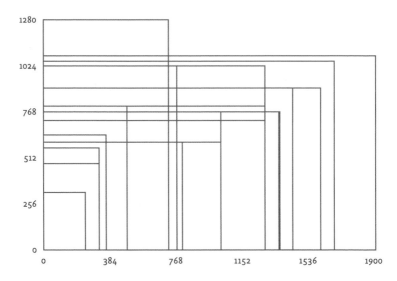

FIG 0.2: Wildly varying screen sizes of the top twenty most popular devices (http://bkaprt.com/rrd/0-06/).

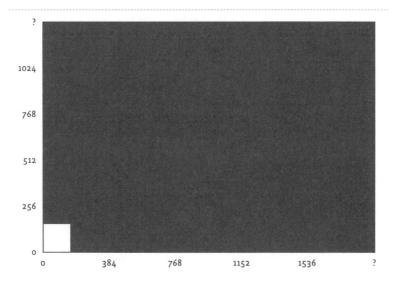

FIG 0.3: Viewport size fragmentation on the web, redrawn from a tweet by Cennydd Bowles (http://bkaprt.com/rrd/0-07/).

FIG 0.4: Ethan Marcotte's example of a responsive layout from his *A List Apart* article (http://bkaprt.com/rrd/0-08/).

In 2010, Ethan Marcotte coined the term responsive web design to describe an approach to web layout that combines fluid grids, fluid images, and CSS3 media queries to deliver layouts that respond (downright magically) to their environment (**FIG 0.4**).

If this book's title led you to believe that responsive web design is not responsible, now is a good time to clarify. Responsive web design is responsible web design. The end. Thank you for reading!

Okay, seriously, I'll explain.

Marcotte's clever combination of web standards technologies gives us a sustainable way to deliver cross-device visual layouts. But Marcotte would be the first to emphasize that responsive layout is one of many variables we must consider when building multi-device sites and applications. Layouts are the start. We need to expand beyond the viewport and consider how we support myriad device capabilities, how we retain accessibility in complex interfaces, and how we deliver assets over the wire.

As Trent Walton says in his essay "Device Agnostic": "Like cars designed to perform in extreme heat or on icy roads, websites should be built to face the reality of the web's inherent variability" (http://bkaprt.com/rrd/0-09/). Thankfully, being responsive from a layout perspective does not preclude us from being responsive from a performance, interactivity, or accessibility perspective.

Responsive and responsible

To deliver on the promise of a broadly accessible, delightful, and sustainable web, we need to combine responsive design with additional responsible practices. A responsible responsive design equally considers the following throughout a project:

- **Usability**: The way a website's user interface is presented to the user, and how that UI responds to browsing conditions and user interactions.
- **Access**: The ability for users of all devices, browsers, and assistive technologies to access and understand a site's features and content.
- **Sustainability**: The ability for the technology driving a site or application to work for devices that exist today and to continue to be usable and accessible to users, devices, and browsers in the future.
- **Performance**: The speed at which a site's features and content are perceived to be delivered to the user and the efficiency with which they operate within the user interface.

That's comprehensive, no? While I ponder renaming this book *Welcome to the Internet by Scott,* let's take a deeper look at some challenges we face in delivering responsibly.

Designing for usability: sensors, input mechanisms, and interactivity

Gone are the days of building websites that only need to work with a mouse (if those days ever existed). We need to care about things like touch, keyboard, stylus, and more—which we may

FIG 0.5: The Windows 8 OS runs on devices that support several input modes, from touch to mouse to keyboard. Photograph by Kārlis Dambrāns (http://bkaprt.com/rrd/0-10/).

encounter in a mix of mobile devices, tablets, or laptops. Many of the most popular devices we use now support touch interactivity. For instance, the Windows 8 operating system supports touch interaction on both laptops and tablets (**FIG 0.5**). Microsoft Kinect tracks hand and arm gestures in midair (**FIG 0.6**). In response to these new input mechanisms, we can't rely solely on traditional mouse cursor interactions like hover; instead, our interfaces must be ready to respond to various input mechanisms within our multi-device universe.

A disparity often exists between powerful native applications and the limited APIs we see on the web and, in truth, that can be a barrier to building web-based applications. Fortunately, many browsers are quickly gaining access to native operating system features like GPS location, contacts, calendar, notifications, file systems, and the camera. These standardized interfaces allow us to communicate with local device features without using plugins like Flash or Java, which rarely work across devices anyhow. In addition to local data APIs, browsers are increasingly able

FIG 0.6: The Microsoft Kinect tracks full-body movement, which may hint at future interactive models for the web. Photograph by Scott and Elaine van der Chijs (http://bkaprt.com/rrd/0-11/).

to access information from device sensors like proximity, GPS, accelerometer, battery levels, and even ambient light. With each new feature, the web platform gains a foothold.

Building for access: considering assistive technology and cross-device continuity

Because assistive technologies increasingly come preinstalled on devices, we often need to take steps to ensure that our sites retain their meaning when browsed in non-visual contexts. Now standard on all Apple computers and iOS devices, screen-reading software VoiceOver sits atop the browser and provides gesture-based navigation as it reads a page aloud. Its multitouch rotor-gesture system offers ways to navigate the web via things like headings and links, which gives us more reasons to be vigilant about the markup we use to communicate our content (**FIG 0.7**).

FIG 0.7: VoiceOver rotor on the iPhone (http://bkaprt.com/rrd/0-12/).

Assistive technology isn't only for those with permanent disabilities; voice and audio may be the preferred and safest interaction modes for any user in certain circumstances. Perhaps the most widely used screen reader is Apple's Siri, which is handy for people who are temporarily unable to look at their screen (while driving, for example) or prefer the convenience of voice interaction over touch typing. As web applications continue to make inroads on our native operating systems, we can expect that software like this will only become more prevalent.

Beyond delivering a usable experience in isolated contexts, we should keep in mind that people increasingly hop from one device to another and expect consistently accessible content. The 2012 Google study *The New Multi-Screen World* revealed that people use multiple devices throughout a single day, in many cases to complete a single task (FIG 0.8). The study found that 65% of shoppers who add an item to their cart on a handheld device later complete their transaction on a laptop computer. Perhaps the shoppers were interrupted by a call or preferred to go through the checkout process on a device with a keyboard. Whatever the reason, we must meet our users wherever they happen to be.

FIG 0.8: Google's 2012 study *The New Multi-Screen World* (http://bkaprt.com/rrd/0-13/).

Browsers: what's old is new again

While modern browsers like Google Chrome, Firefox, and, yes, even Internet Explorer press ahead with new features, many devices in the wild and in stores are locked into browsers that are no longer in development. For example, version 2 of the Android operating system continues to be incredibly popular worldwide, despite being more than two major releases behind the latest and including a built-in browser that hasn't seen updates since 2011 (http://bkaprt.com/rrd/0-14/)! Seasoned (read: old) developers like me may recall a similar situation with IE6's drawn-out reign. Unfortunately, long-term support of browser versions is inevitably cut in favor of the next new platform or a company's shifted priorities, leaving existing users in the lurch.

Browser lock-in presents challenges, then—but also opportunities. Users often seek out other browsers for their platforms, some of which offer unusual features and selling points. For example, millions of people who prefer web pages that load faster and consume less of their data plans (crazy, right?) choose a browser like Opera Mini, which requests web content through remote proxy servers that optimize each page's download size (**FIG 0.9**). Proxy-based browsers support little or no JavaScript

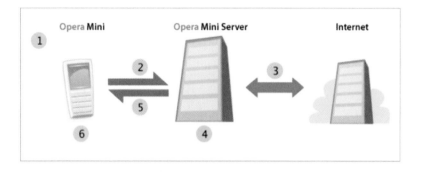

FIG 0.9: An Opera infographic demonstrating how the Opera Mini browser accesses the web (http://bkaprt.com/rrd/0-15/).

interactivity on the device itself; ironically, practices that benefit older browsers, such as delivering functional HTML, also help the millions running these new proxy browsers!

Prioritizing performance: networks, weight, and performance impact

Mobile network constraints grow more nuanced and challenging, even as they slowly improve as a whole. In the meantime, network connections are intermittent and lagging even in developed countries. To ensure high performance, we must reassess the ways we deliver our assets, reduce the weight and number of those assets, and remove potential points of failure that block access to our content.

Any unused code we deliver wastes our users' time and money, and we have plenty of room for improvement. In his April 2013 post "What are Responsive Websites Made Of?," Guy Podjarny evaluated file transfer sizes of 500 responsive websites and found that 86% sent roughly equivalent assets to all viewport sizes (http://bkaprt.com/rrd/0-16/). Rather than serving optimized images, for example, sites were delivering large-screen images (thus relying on browsers to scale them down for smaller screens), along with plenty of CSS, JavaScript, and other assets that were only necessary in some contexts.

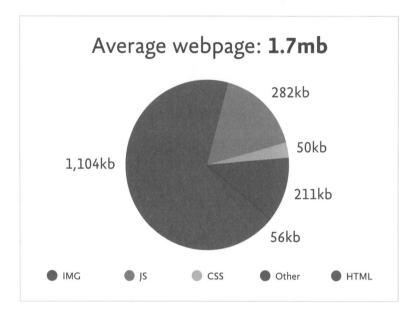

Average webpage: 1.7mb

282kb

50kb

211kb

56kb

1,104kb

IMG　　JS　　CSS　　Other　　HTML

FIG 0.10: Average website weight, April 2014 (http://bkaprt.com/rrd/0-17/).

Of course, the web's burgeoning weight problem isn't exclusive to responsive design. It has festered in the fixed-desktop web for some time; as of April 2014, the average website weighed a whopping 1.7 megabytes (FIG 0.10).

Unoptimized, heavy websites can mean long load times for users. A 2012 StrangeLoop survey of the Alexa Top 2000 sites showed that the average load time was six to ten seconds in Internet Explorer 7 with a Wi-Fi connection (never mind how slow it may be on a mobile connection) (FIG 0.11)! The cost of poor performance translates directly to users and, as a result, to businesses. In 2012, Walmart found that for every second shaved off load time, it gained 2% in conversions; incremental revenue went up 1% with each 100 millisecond decrease (http://bkaprt.com/rrd/0-18/).

In addition, as cell network speeds and reliability continue to constrain mobile use, the cost of data itself has become more prohibitive. If you purchased an iPhone from the Apple store

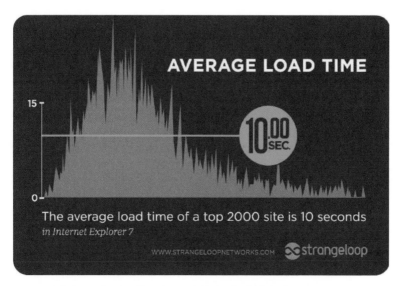

AVERAGE LOAD TIME

15

10.00 SEC.

0

The average load time of a top 2000 site is 10 seconds
in Internet Explorer 7

WWW.STRANGELOOPNETWORKS.COM strangeloop

FIG 0.11: A site's transfer size affects how quickly (or slowly) it loads (http://bkaprt.com/rrd/0-19/).

in the United States in 2014, the cheapest Verizon plan at $60/ month netted you only 250 megabytes of data. In light of that 1.7-megabyte average page weight, it's easy to see how quickly your monthly quota is spent.

Because responsible network use is so vital to performance, this book dedicates entire chapters to minimizing our delivery weights *and* optimizing the ways we deliver code so that sites are usable as fast as possible.

Embracing unpredictability

The web has always been a hostile design medium. As multi-device use rises, scenarios like low bandwidth, small screens, unpredictable screen orientation, or non-visual browsing aren't exceptions anymore; they're everyday contexts. Designing for an inflexible set of conditions leads to problems for our users: the interfaces we design and develop are increasingly interacted with in ways we can neither predict nor control.

To deliver on today's web successfully, we must think responsively down to the smallest detail and prepare our code to counter the unexpected. And to do that, we need to consider both past and possible usage patterns. The need for responsive sites that prioritize performance, access, usability, and sustainability is clear, but executing on those goals is no easy task. Throughout this book, we'll explore the challenges we face as we implement responsive design. By following responsible practices and patterns, we can eliminate many accessibility and performance issues before they occur to deliver appropriate, optimized experiences, regardless of a browser's features and constraints.

Our goal is to create delightful, inclusive experiences—a tall order—so let's forge ahead and get acquainted with some approaches to the challenges we face.

RESPONSIBLE DESIGN

" My love for responsive centers around the idea that my website will meet you wherever you are—from mobile to full-blown desktop and anywhere in between."
—TRENT WALTON, "Fit To Scale" (http://bkaprt.com/rrd/1-01/)

RESPONSIVE DESIGN'S core tenets (fluid grids, fluid images, and media queries) go a long way toward providing a holistic package for cross-device interface design. But responsive design itself relies on features that may not work as expected—or at all. Our sites need to react to unexpected user behaviors, network conditions, and unique support scenarios.

In this chapter, we'll dig into two responsible tenets: usability and accessibility. We'll cover higher-level considerations before getting into nitty-gritty code you can implement now and expect to last. To start, let's talk design.

DESIGNING FOR USABILITY

When we consider usability in responsive design, we think about how to present a design's content and features across a range of screen sizes and devices. Do the interface components yield to the content when screen real estate is tight? Do the components function intuitively in response to various input modes? Are the content and hierarchy easy to parse? Do the line lengths foster readability across screen sizes?

Get into the browser quickly

"Let's change the phrase 'designing in the browser' to 'deciding in the browser.'"
—DAN MALL, The Pastry Box Project (http://bkaprt.com/rrd/1-02/)

At Filament Group, we start most of our projects in Adobe Illustrator, where we iterate on high-level visual design concepts. We then try to move to code as soon as possible. At this stage, we aim to design the fewest number of interface variations that communicate a plan for layout and interactivity across viewports—mere suggestions for how the site will look and feel on any given device. Decisions about how features react to different input mechanisms and browser capabilities, as well as the particular viewport sizes that should receive each layout variation, remain to be determined. The goal is to move into the browser as quickly as we can to make design and interaction decisions in context, which translates to more informed recommendations for our clients.

Find your breakpoints

The viewport sizes at which we change from one fluid layout to another using media queries are called *breakpoints*. Here are two examples:

```
/* first breakpoint */
@media (min-width: 520px){
    ...styles for 520px widths and up go here!
}
/* second breakpoint */
@media (min-width: 735px){
    ...styles for 735px widths and up go here!
}
```

While it's tempting to choose breakpoints early in the design process, perhaps based on the dimensions of popular devices we know we need to support, the truth is that we shouldn't choose breakpoints at all. Instead, we should find them, using our content as a guide.

"Start with the small screen first, then expand until it looks like shit. TIME FOR A BREAKPOINT!"
—**STEPHEN HAY**, http://bkaprt.com/rrd/1-03/

A layout's design and content should shape and inform a layout's breakpoints. As Hay notes, the easiest way to find breakpoints is simply to resize the browser viewport until the content becomes awkward (that's the technical term) to use or read—and presto, a breakpoint.

In addition to a gut check, you might opt for a slightly more objective guideline. Per Richard Rutter's homage to Robert Bringhurst, *The Elements of Typographic Style Applied to the Web* (http://bkaprt.com/rrd/1-05/), an optimal *measure*—the number of characters per line in a column of text—for immersive reading is widely thought to fall between 45 and 75 characters, including spaces (**FIG 1.1**). If you're resizing a layout outward, watch for when a column of text approaches that range: it's probably a good place to adjust your layout.

As you work with complex responsive designs, you'll find that breakpoints often occur at different times for different portions of a layout, and that some are more significant than others.

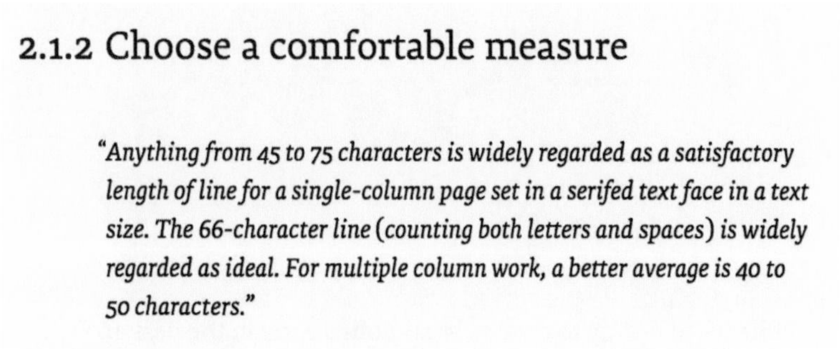

2.1.2 Choose a comfortable measure

"Anything from 45 to 75 characters is widely regarded as a satisfactory length of line for a single-column page set in a serifed text face in a text size. The 66-character line (counting both letters and spaces) is widely regarded as ideal. For multiple column work, a better average is 40 to 50 characters."

FIG 1.1: Here, a seventy-character line length makes for comfortable reading (http://bkaprt.com/rrd/1-04/).

Major breakpoints mark big shifts, usually to add columns or dramatically change the presentation of more than one component; *minor* breakpoints involve smaller design tweaks (such as changing a component's font-size to prevent text wrapping) that take full advantage of the spaces between the major breakpoints. In general, I find that major layout breakpoints are decided early in development, while minor ones act as finishing touches. The fewer breakpoints we use, the easier a responsive design will be to maintain.

Let's look at an example. On the *Boston Globe* website, we have two or three major layout breakpoints, but the more complicated components break more often. The site's masthead component has four major breakpoints, as well as some minor ones for slight adjustments to prevent text wrapping (**FIG 1.2**).

Design modularly
As in the masthead example, I find it helpful to compile the multiple configurations of each modular component in isolation; that way, I can test its usability and document its variations in one place. Developer Dave Rupert of Paravel explored this concept in his post "Responsive Deliverables" (http://bkaprt.com/rrd/1-06/). "Responsive deliverables should look a lot like fully

 Major

First breakpoint: navigation and search options toggle on tap.

 Major

Second breakpoint: logo moves left to split the width with the navigation.

 Major

Third breakpoint: logo moves back to center, search box visible at all times.

 Major

Fourth breakpoint: search box moves left of logo, navigation expands.

 Minor

Final breakpoint: search box widens, classified links visible at all times on top left.

FIG 1.2: Major and minor breakpoints of the Boston Globe's masthead.

functioning Twitter Bootstrap-style (http://bkaprt.com/rrd/1-07/) systems custom tailored for your clients' needs," Rupert writes. In other words, we should build and document our components from the inside out, as standalone pieces that play nicely with others.

Same content, reduced noise

You've figured out how to find horizontal breakpoints across a range of viewport sizes. How do you fit all that content on small screens without making things noisy? Responsive design has (undeservedly) received a bad rap because of sites that attempt to avoid messy situations by hiding parts of the content from users—denying access to content that was ostensibly important enough to include in the first place. Remember, if it's useful to some people, it's likely useful to everyone. As Luke Wroblewski's book *Mobile First* instructs, rather than hide content that's inconvenient to display, it's best to reorganize the design to retain usability on smaller viewports.

Fortunately, we have many design patterns that work around small-screen constraints in interesting, intuitive, and responsible ways.

Progressive disclosure

One such pattern is *progressive disclosure*, a fancy term for showing content on demand. To be clear, not all hiding is bad; it's only bad if the user has no way to access the hidden content. The idea behind progressive disclosure is simple: hide portions of content, but provide interface cues so that users can view it when they wish (**FIG 1.3**).

Progressive disclosure is most often a simple show-and-hide like the example above, but we have plenty of ways to visually toggle content. For instance, this property listing component does a 3D flip upon tap or click to reveal additional information about a property, such as its address and location on a map (**FIG 1.4**). For browsers without 3D CSS animation support, users can toggle to the map without an animated transition, while basic browsers display the map at all times, just beneath the property information.

Off-canvas layout, a term coined by Luke Wroblewski in his article "Off-Canvas Multi-Device Layouts," describes another notable approach to minimizing complexity on small screens

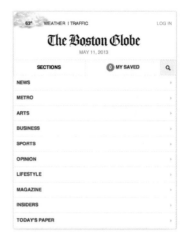

FIG 1.3: *Boston Globe*'s navigation uses progressive disclosure on small viewports.

(http://bkaprt.com/rrd/1-08/). Wroblewski documents several patterns for positioning lower-priority interface components offscreen until users cue them by tapping a menu icon or similar item; the formerly offscreen content then enters the viewport, overlapping or pushing aside the primary content (FIG 1.5). This on-demand approach is becoming common in small-screen layouts.

Responsive tables

Tabular data is one of the toughest content types to present on a small screen. It's often essential that the user see column and

FIG 1.4: Progressively disclosed content flips in 3D to display more information.

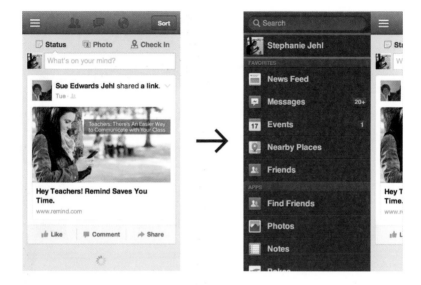

FIG 1.5: Tapping the menu icon reveals Facebook's off-canvas navigation from the screen's left edge.

row headers associated with a table cell, and yet we can only fit so many rows and columns on screen (**FIG 1.6**).

At Filament, we experimented a lot and found a couple of patterns that worked well enough to include in the jQuery Mobile framework. The first pattern, Reflow (http://bkaprt.com/rrd/1-09/), reformats the table from a multi-column view to a list view; each cell becomes its own row, with a row header to its left. (**FIG 1.7**).

To pull this off, Reflow uses CSS to set each cell in the table to `display: block`, creating a new row, and JavaScript to grab each of the table's column headers and insert them in each cell to serve as the labels (while hiding the additional labels from screen readers). Reflow suits simple tables that act like formatted lists, but its small-screen presentation falls short when you need to compare data points across rows.

FIG 1.6: Large tables can cause usability trouble on small screens.

Rank	Movie Title			Year	Rating	Reviews
Rank	1	1	Citizen Kane	1941	100%	74
Movie Title	Citizen Kane	2	Casablanca	1942	97%	64
Year	1941	3	The Godfather	1972	97%	87
Rating	100%	4	Gone with the Wind	1939	96%	87
Reviews	74	5	Lawrence of Arabia	1962	94%	87
		6	Dr. Strangelove Or How I Learned to Stop Worrying and Love the Bomb	1964	92%	74
Rank	2	7	The Graduate	1967	91%	122
Movie Title	Casablanca	8	The Wizard of Oz	1939	90%	72
Year	1942	9	Singin' in the Rain	1952	89%	85
Rating	97%	10	Inception	2010	84%	78

FIG 1.7: An example of the jQuery Mobile Reflow table pattern, with the same table shown at narrow and wide widths.

FIG 1.8: An example of the jQuery mobile Column Toggle table pattern, with the same table shown at narrow and wide widths.

The Column Toggle (http://bkaprt.com/rrd/1-10/) pattern picks up that slack. It works by selectively showing columns in a table as horizontal space allows. If there isn't room, CSS hides the column data, but a menu offers users the chance to override the CSS and display the column anyway, eventually causing the table to expand wide enough to warrant horizontal scrolling (**FIG 1.8**).

These are only two of the numerous potential patterns for responsibly presenting tabular content. For more examples, check out Brad Frost's project Responsive Patterns (http://bkaprt.com/rrd/1-11/). You'll find everything from horizontal navigation components that collapse into menus when space is tight to CSS-Flexbox-driven grids for complex page layouts.

DESIGNING FOR TOUCH (AND EVERYTHING ELSE)

A responsive layout is but one step. Even if your site flows beautifully from one screen size to the next, you're not doing your job if someone can't *use* it. Touch isn't only the domain of small screens; many devices offer touch alongside other input mechanisms. But as the number of people on touch devices surges, we must add touch to our arsenal of common interactions like mouse, focus, and keyboard. While the intricacies of touch can be daunting, we don't need to completely overhaul our designs to be touch-friendly. Far from it: one of the joys of responsible design is how it builds on our everyday tool set. Two basic measures pack a wallop on the usability of an existing, mouse-based interface:

- Make sure any content that offers mouse-centric interactivity (like hover) is also accessible in browsers where a mouse pointer may not exist.
- Don't assume touch will be used, but design as if it will be. Let's see how these play out with the following considerations.

Save hover for shortcuts

The absence of mouseover (or hover) interactions is one of the biggest changes when learning to support touch. In fact, the lack of mouseover support on many touch devices is a primary reason that many sites designed for the desktop web falter in touch contexts, resulting in usability problems that prevent users from accessing certain features. You can't rely on mouseover for vital design interactions, but you can use it as a nice-to-have alternate way to reach otherwise accessible content.

One example is the navigation for the Global News Canada website, designed by Upstatement and developed by the Filament Group team (FIG 1.9). The global navigation links users to National, Locals, and Watch section homepages when clicked or tapped. These links also feature split-button drop menus that toggle between sections on hover. On a touch screen, one tap directly sends users to that section's homepage, so we came up with an alternative mechanism to toggle between menus and account for all breakpoints. The split buttons with arrows next to each navigation link do just that, offering tap or click access to the drop menus.

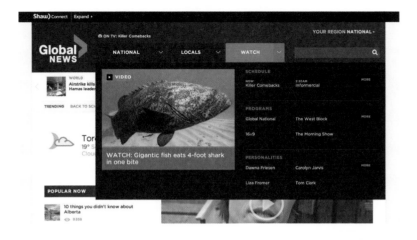

FIG 1.9: The split-button menus on GlobalNews.ca work for touch and mouseover.

Keep in touch

One rule of thumb(s): the devices accessing your site may or may not have touch screens, but always design as if they will. Fingers aren't precise, so we need to enlarge button and link target areas to make them easier to tap. How much bigger is an open discussion, though Apple's guidelines suggest 44 × 44 pixels as the minimum size for usable buttons. Based on findings from MIT's Touch Lab (http://bkaprt.com/rrd/1-12/), the *Smashing Magazine* article "Finger-Friendly Design: Ideal Mobile Touchscreen Target Sizes" by author Anthony T suggests slightly larger targets at 45-57 pixels, and 72 pixels for buttons for thumb use, like the ones located near the bottom of a handheld device's screen (FIG 1.10).

Don't forget your white space! Equally important as the size of touchable elements is the space around those elements. A smaller button surrounded by dead space can be as easy to use as a larger element, so the size of the button within its tappable footprint becomes a question of visual emphasis.

57 Pixel Touch Target
Index finger fits snugly inside. Target edges
give visual feedback. Finger pad is used
instead of fingertip.

72 Pixel Touch Target
Thumb fits snugly inside. Target edges
give visual feedback. Thumb pad is used
instead of thumb tip.

FIG 1.10: Illustrations from *Smashing Magazine*'s article (http://bkaprt.com/rrd/1-13/).

The usual gestures

Touch screens offer the potential for richer interactions than tap alone—many touch gestures have become commonplace, particularly in native apps. This diagram by Craig Villamor, Dan Willis, and Luke Wroblewski demonstrates some popular gestures in touch interaction (**FIG 1.11**).

You're probably familiar with most of these gestures, which are used by operating systems on several devices (including iOS). Within browsers, these gestures are often paired with convenient default behavior that varies from device to device; some gestures share the same behavior. For example, a double tap or pinch or spread in iOS Safari causes the browser to zoom in or out on a particular region. Dragging or flicking in any direction causes the page to scroll; and a press, or touch-hold, often exposes a context menu akin to what you'd see when right-clicking with a mouse.

Native gestures like these have all sorts of implications for how we can responsibly develop for touch. Users form expectations about their devices' native features, so we don't want to disable or repurpose a feature like touch-hold if we can avoid it. While browsers do let us use touch events like `touchstart`, `touchmove`, and `touchend` (or the new standard pointer events `pointerdown`, `pointermove`, `pointerup`, etc.) to specify gestures with JavaScript, how can we do so without conflicting with native touch behavior?

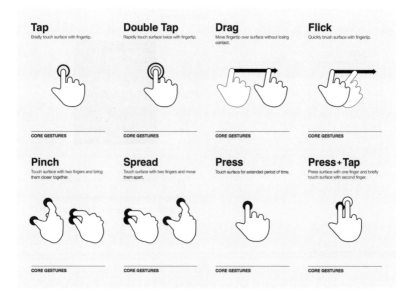

Tap
Briefly touch surface with fingertip.

Double Tap
Rapidly touch surface twice with fingertip.

Drag
Move fingertip over surface without losing contact.

Flick
Quickly brush surface with fingertip.

CORE GESTURES CORE GESTURES CORE GESTURES CORE GESTURES

Pinch
Touch surface with two fingers and bring them closer together.

Spread
Touch surface with two fingers and move them apart.

Press
Touch surface for extended period of time.

Press+Tap
Press surface with one finger and briefly touch surface with second finger.

CORE GESTURES CORE GESTURES CORE GESTURES CORE GESTURES

FIG 1.11: Touch Gesture diagram (http://bkaprt.com/rrd/1-14/).

Web-safe gestures: do they exist?

Let's compile a list of web-safe gestures we can use in our sites (spoiler: it's short). Based on the native gestures in today's popular devices, we have tap, two-finger tap, horizontal drag, and horizontal flick. Yet within this small list, we still have potential for conflict. For instance, Chrome on iOS and Android allows users to horizontally swipe to switch between open tabs, while iOS Safari uses the same gesture to go back or forward in browser history, which means our use of those gestures can lead to unexpected behavior. Horizontal drag gestures can also introduce issues even in touch browsers that don't use them for native navigation. For example, if a page's content stretches wider than the browser's viewport, which often happens after zooming in, a horizontal touch-drag is typically used to scroll the page right or left, so we have to be careful that our custom touch gestures don't interfere.

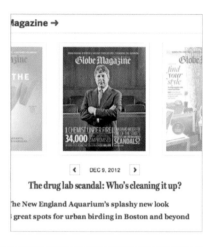

FIG 1.12: The multiple-input-mode carousels on the *Boston Globe* site.

Keep in mind that I've deemed these gestures safe only because I'm unaware of any touch-based browsers that use them—yet. The moment iOS implements two-finger tap, anything we've built may conflict with native behavior, and that's not future-friendly at all. This doesn't mean we should avoid building custom gestures, but it highlights the importance of developing for many input modes. If one fails for any reason, we'll have alternate ways to access our content.

In practice, this means ensuring there's always a click-and-keyboard-based interface for interaction. For example, the carousel of magazine covers on the *Boston Globe* site has several interactive options (**FIG 1.12**). You can click the arrows beneath the carousel, click the covers to the right or left of the featured image, use the right and left arrow keys on your keyboard, or touch-drag the carousel on a touch device. Think of touch gestures as a nice-to-have enhancement on top of broadly supported input modes.

Perhaps a bigger problem with touch gestures is discovery, as touch gestures often lack any visual interface to hint at their presence. We ran into this dilemma when building the *Boston Globe*'s saved articles feature, which allows you to save articles to your account so you can read them later. On small screens, the Save buttons hide by default but can be toggled into view with a

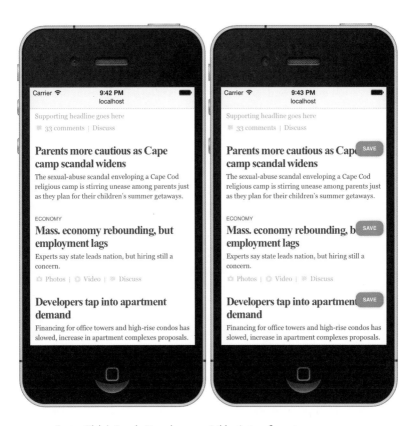

FIG 1.13: *Boston Globe*'s Save buttons become visible via two-finger tap.

two-finger tap (**FIG 1.13**). Of course, there is no easy way to know that unless you visit the help section and read the instructions!

Scripting touch interactivity

Touch-screen browsers are typically capable of using components designed for mouse input, so outside of accommodating touch from a design perspective, you may not need to do anything special with JavaScript to ensure touch support. However, touch-specific events do exist, and the advantage of scripting with them is often a matter of richness and enhancement. When developing components, for example, it's particularly nice to write code that listens for touch events because they respond immediately to touch interaction. By comparison, in many touch browsers, mouse events like `click` and `mouseup` typically fire 300 milliseconds or more after a user taps the screen (the device waits to make sure that a double tap isn't happening before it handles the `click`), so any site that's coded to respond to mouse events alone will suffer minor but noticeable delays. That said, scripting touch gestures can be tricky because most browsers that support touch emit both mouse and touch events whenever a touch occurs. Further complicating things, browsers sometimes use different touch-event names (such as the widely used `touchstart` rather than the emerging standard, `pointerdown`).

Whatever touch-screen optimizations we make, it's crucial not to hinder people's ability to interact with content using non-touch input mechanisms like the mouse and keyboard. A common, responsible approach to ensure that touch interactions work as fast as possible is to set up event listeners for both mouse and touch events. During a particular interaction, the logic would handle whichever event type happens first and ignore the other to prevent the possibility of running any scripting twice. Sounds straightforward, but it's not. That's why I recommend using a well-tested, open-source JavaScript library to do the hard work for you. I use Tappy.js (http://bkaprt.com/rrd/1-15/), a script I created to allow you to listen for a custom `tap` event when writing jQuery code. Here's Tappy in play:

```
$( ".myBtn" ).bind( "tap", function(){
    alert( "tap!" );
});
```

Behind the scenes, that `tap` event is listening for touch, keyboard, or mouse clicks to perform a specific behavior. (In this case, it throws an alert that says, "tap!" I'm sure you can find better uses for it, of course.)

For a library that offers a more advanced set of touch features, check out FastClick (http://bkaprt.com/rrd/1-16/), created and maintained by the talented team at *Financial Times*.

DESIGNING FOR ACCESS

We've covered some major aspects of usability, such as designing for screen variation, finding breakpoints, and handling input modes inclusively. But for components to be usable across devices, we must make sure that they're accessible in browsers that don't support our ideal presentation or behavior, and for users who browse the web with assistive technology. For these reasons and more, you can't do a better service to your users than to start with plain old HTML. A major strength of HTML is its innate backward compatibility, which means pages built with even the latest iterations can still be accessed from almost any HTML-capable device.

While HTML documents are born quite accessible, they don't always stay that way: careless application of CSS and JavaScript can render formerly accessible content completely unusable, leaving users worse off than they were with the initial, bare-bones experience. For example, consider a drop menu whose content is hidden with `display: none;`. With exceptions, screen readers will relay only the content that is presented on screen, so if precautions aren't in place, that menu's content will not only be hidden *visually*, it will also be hidden *audibly* from screen reader users. We must provide meaningful cues to alert all users—not just those browsing the web visually—that the menu content exists and can be shown (or heard) when desired.

As we continue to push HTML toward new interactivity, it's critical that we think of access as something we constantly risk losing, as something we must retain throughout our development process.

Ensure access with progressive enhancement

The idea that the web is born accessible pairs neatly with the concept of progressive enhancement, which advocates starting with functional, meaningful HTML and then unobtrusively layering presentation (CSS) and behavior (JS) on top for a richer, more dynamic user experience.

With power comes responsibility. Any time you venture beyond standard browser rendering of HTML into building

FIG 1.14: A view (left) of the underlying native controls behind an enhanced user interface (right).

your own presentation and interactivity, you're responsible for accessibility. This requires some planning. As developers, we must "see through" our visual interface designs to discover their underlying meaning in HTML.

In Filament Group's book *Designing with Progressive Enhancement,* we describe this process as *the x-ray perspective* (FIG 1.14):

> The x-ray perspective is a methodology we've developed to evaluate a complex site design, break it down to its most basic modular parts, and build it back up in such a way that a single coded page will work for modern browsers with full functional capabilities as well as other browsers and devices that may understand only basic HTML.

The process of x-raying a design's parts may require a certain amount of creative thinking; it depends on how closely a custom control resembles a native equivalent. Some are fairly transparent: say, a button that acts as a checkbox input. In this case, a bit of CSS alone could render some label and input markup

FIG 1.15: A standard input and label styled as a button.

from a standard text and box presentation into the button-like component shown below (**FIG 1.15**):

```
<label class="check">
  <input type="checkbox">Bold
</label>
```

A CSS-alone approach has triple benefits. It's simple, light-weight, and, most important, using native HTML form elements almost guarantees that the control will be accessible to users with disabilities. In other words, assistive technology like Apple's built-in VoiceOver screen reader will read the native control aloud as if the visual enhancements aren't even there: "bold, unchecked checkbox" by default and "bold, checked checkbox" when checked.

Easy, right? However, it can be difficult to maintain this level of accessibility with more complex custom components.

Responsibly enhance a complex control

Let's focus those x-ray specs on something more abstract, such as a slider (**FIG 1.16**):

A great feature in the HTML5 specification is the new set of form input types like number, color, and search. You can safely use these types today to deliver more specialized interactivity in supporting browsers; browsers that don't understand them will simply render the input as a standard text type.

Here's some markup for a color input:

```
<label for="color">Choose a color:</label>
<input type="color" id="color">
```

FIGURE 1.17 shows how it renders in Google Chrome, a supporting browser.

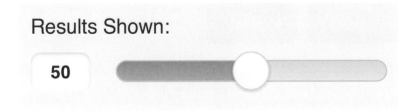

Results Shown:

50

FIG 1.16: A custom slider control with a numerical input.

Choose a color:

FIG 1.17: A color input with a color picker in Google Chrome.

FIGURE 1.18 shows it in iOS 7, a non-supporting browser.

Another new form input is range, which displays a slider control in most browsers. But the generated native slider leaves a lot to be desired from a design and usability perspective. For one, its appearance is vexing—sometimes impossible—to customize. Depending on the browser, the native slider lacks any text label to display the slider's value, making it useless for choosing precise values. For example, **FIGURE 1.19** shows how a native range input with possible values of 0-10 renders in iOS 7 Safari.

```
<label for="value">Choose a value:</label>
<input type="range" id="value" min="0" max="10">
```

FIG 1.18: A color input falls back to a plain text input in iOS 7.

Choose a value:

FIG 1.19: A range input rendered in iOS 7 Safari, which gives no feedback about minimum, maximum, or current value.

Unless we're designing a music-volume control, this slider isn't helpful. If we want to create a usable, touch-friendly slider, we'll need to build it ourselves. Let's do so in a way that works for everyone.

Results Shown: 61

The first and most important step is to start with our pal, HTML. Deep down, a slider is a visualization of a numeric scale, so let's begin with an input element and give it a type of number, which is another HTML5 input that degrades to a text input in non-supporting browsers. Using number has the benefit of allowing us to use several standard, complementary attributes that shape the control's constraints: min and max. We'll use these attributes as our HTML starting point (**FIG 1.20**):

```
<label for="results">Results Shown:</label>
<input type="number" id="results" name="results" »
  value="60" min="0" max="100" />
```

Now that we have our foundation, we can use JavaScript to create a slider component that will manipulate the input's value when the user drags its handle.

The actual scripting to pull that off lies beyond this book's scope, but I will cover the resulting generated markup and how to make sure the slider doesn't hinder accessibility. First, the newly generated markup in bold:

```
<label for="results">Results Shown:</label>
<input type="number" id="results" name="results" »
  value="60" min="0" max="100" />
<div class="slider">
  <a href="#" class="handle" style="left: 60%;"></a>
</div>
```

Let's walk through the changes. To create our slider handle and track, we need to use an element that is natively focusable via keyboard, in this case an a element, to which I assigned the

Results Shown:

61

FIG 1.21: Our slider div, with the input element shown to the left.

class handle for reference. We also need a div container element for the .handle to be visually styled as a slider track. As a user drags the handle or taps their arrow keys, we use JavaScript to manipulate the handle's CSS left positioning with a percentage that reflects the distance the user has dragged, and update the value of our input control as well. I've included our new slider markup in bold (**FIG 1.21**):

```
<label for="results">Results Shown:</label>
<input type="number" id="results" name="results" »
  value="61" min="0" max="100" />
<div class="slider">
  <a href="#" class="handle" style="left: 61%;"></a>
</div>
```

CSS styling aside, that's the bulk of the behavior a basic slider control needs to perform. But our work isn't done. Our page started out accessible, but with JavaScript we've introduced markup that's playing an unnatural role—that anchor element with a class of .handle. When a screen reader encounters this element, it will read it aloud as "number link" because it appears to be an ordinary link with an href value of #.

To prevent this markup from leading to a confusing experience, we have two options: we can either hide the slider from screen readers (since the text input already exists) or do additional work to make the slider itself meaningful to screen readers. I prefer the simplicity of hiding the new control; all we need to do is add an aria-hidden attribute to the div, which tells a screen reader to ignore the contents of that element when reading the page aloud:

```
<label for="results">Results Shown:</label>
<input type="range" id="results" name="results" »
  value="61" min="0" max="100" />
<div class="slider" aria-hidden>
  <a href="#" style="left: 61%;"></a>
</div>
```

Just like that, we've progressively enhanced our input into a better visual presentation without undermining accessibility. "But... ARIA *what?*" you may ask. Briefly, the W3C's Accessible Rich Internet Applications (ARIA) specification is a set of HTML attributes that embed semantic meaning in HTML elements that play a non-native role—whether that's an a acting as a menu button instead of a link (which would use ARIA's role="button" attribute) or a ul acting as a navigable tree component (the role="tree" attribute), as you'd see when browsing a list of files in an operating system window. There's even an ARIA role to describe a slider, if we wanted to go that route with our component above: role="slider". In addition to those role-based attributes, ARIA provides *state* attributes that describe the state a control is in, such as aria-expanded, aria-collapsed, and aria-hidden (used above), and even attributes to describe the current and possible values of a custom slider control. Find out more about ARIA over at the W3C's site (http://bkaprt.com/rrd/1-17/).

Make data visualizations accessible

Data visualizations, like charts and graphs, are often delivered in ways that aren't terribly meaningful for those using assistive technology. For example, take a complex line chart in a *New York Times* article, delivered via an img element (**FIG 1.22**).

To a screen reader, all of the information in this chart is invisible. Now, a responsible developer might (at the very least!) go as far as adding an alt attribute to describe the chart's data, but such data can be impossible for a single string of text to describe meaningfully:

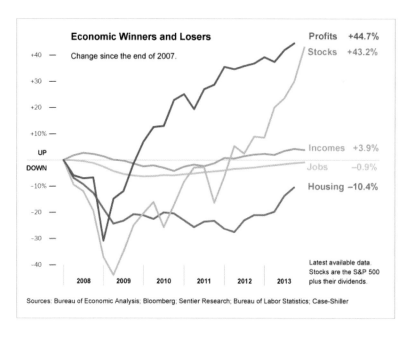

FIG 1.22: This complex line chart was delivered via an img element (http://bkaprt.com/rrd/1-18/).

```
<img src="chart.png" alt="Economic winners and losers, »
  Change since...">
```

How can we communicate this better? Ready those x-ray specs. As we did with the slider, perhaps we could choose a more meaningful starting point from which to create this graph. Consider the pie chart in FIGURE 1.23, for example. How might we build it in a way that provides more meaning to screen readers than an img tag can?

We can start with HTML that's meaningful to all users and present the chart as an enhancement. By peering through the chart to its underlying meaning, we might discover that a chart's bones could be described with an HTML table element. We

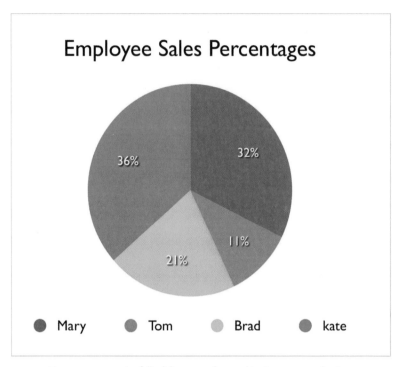

FIG 1.23: How can we meaningfully deliver complex graphics to screen readers?

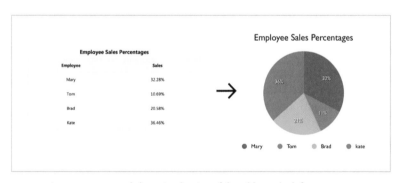

FIG 1.24: A canvas-generated chart visualization of the table on the left.

could then parse the HTML markup below with JavaScript to dynamically draw the chart with a technology like HTML5's `canvas` or SVG. Once the chart is generated, we might even choose to accessibly hide the table by positioning it off screen, deeming the chart a visual improvement over the table it replaces (**FIG 1.24**).

```
<table>
  <summary>Employee Sales Percentages</summary>
  <tr>
    <th>Employee</th>
    <th>Sales</th>
  </tr>
  <tr>
    <td>Mary</td>
    <td>32.28%</td>
  </tr>
  <tr>
    <td>Tom</td>
    <td>10.69%</td>
  </tr>
  <tr>
    <td>Brad</td>
    <td>20.58%</td>
  </tr>
  <tr>
    <td>Kate</td>
    <td>36.46%</td>
  </tr>
</table>
```

We've only scratched the surface of everything we should consider when building accessible, complex interfaces. But it's hard to go wrong when starting with markup that is valid, accessible, and functional on almost any device, and layer enhancements from there. It's a fine line between an enhancement and a hindrance, one that we as responsible developers must carefully walk.

Building this way is a clear win for access, but planning for such variation makes for an interesting challenge when it comes to communicating these expectations to our clients and QA testers. Perhaps a tweak to how we define support is in order...

An enhanced support strategy

In the article "Grade Components, Not Browsers," I expanded on a great idea by my colleague Maggie Wachs about defining support granularly for each site component (rather than assigning a grade to a browser as a whole, as is common with approaches like Yahoo's Graded Browser Support) (http://bkaprt. com/rrd/1-19/). The documentation we share with our clients assigns graded levels for each component based on its major tiers of enhancement.

As an example, the following image shows enhancement levels for a property detail component on a real estate website (**FIG 1.25**). The enhancement level that a browser receives depends on several conditions, such as support of features like Ajax and 3D CSS Transform.

This documentation accomplishes a few things. For one, it helps us to itemize for our clients the particular conditions that enable portions of their site to work at an enhanced level, so everyone (designers, clients, and quality assurance testers) knows what to expect. It also acts as a reminder that some components may receive a higher grade than others, depending on the browser. In other words, feature support varies across even modern browsers, so a browser may receive a bells-and-whistles A-grade experience for one component and a less-enhanced B-grade experience for another.

When we document support this way, we shift the focus from the browser to its features and constraints. We start to think of support as less a binary switch—or even a scale—than a scatter plot. In this system, every browser that understands HTML is supported and is guaranteed access to the site's primary features and content. As Jeremy Keith points out: "It's our job to

Property detail component

Graded experiences

Grade C: Basic formatting, link to map

Grade B: Same formatting, interactive map in page
Requires: JavaScript, Ajax Support

Grade A: Same formatting, map revealed with 3D flip
Requires: CSS 3D transform support

FIG 1.25: A graded documentation of a feature whose presentation varies across browsers.

explain how the web works...and how the unevenly-distributed nature of browser capabilities is not a bug, it's a feature" (http://bkaprt.com/rrd/1-20/).

Speaking of features, we need reliable, device-agnostic, and sustainable ways to detect them. Let's move on to look at the why and the how of doing so.

2 SUSTAINABLE DETECTION

GIVEN THE DIVERSE NATURE of browsers today, the ability to detect browser features and constraints is vital to delivering an appropriate user experience. We have many ways to approach this detection, some more responsible than others.

DEVICE DETECTION: THE EVOLUTION OF A STOPGAP

Among topics of great debate in web development, perhaps the most contentious is the practice of device detection. Its mere mention in a gathering of peers gets my stomach tingling in anticipation of the fiery opinions that await. In truth, a little device detection is sometimes necessary in a complex cross-device codebase, but with each site I build, I find fewer reasons to use it.

This is a good thing, as any approach that includes device-specific logic risks threatening the sustainability of our codebase in the long term. Let's explore some reasons why that is.

Detecting all the things

When a user first requests a page, we know precious little about their browsing environment. We don't know the size of their device's screen, or if their device even has a screen. We don't know their browser's capabilities. Fortunately, we can detect these qualities after delivering code to the browser, but in some cases that's later than we'd prefer.

One thing we can universally detect upon first arrival is a browser's user agent information, included in every request that a browser—or user agent—makes. This string of text packs a variety of information, including the browser's make and version, like Firefox 14 or Chrome 25, and its operating system, like Apple iOS. Crafty developers realized early on that if they gathered data about various browsers and their capabilities and stored them on their server (in what's known as a device database), they could query that information when a user visits their site to get a good idea of the sort of browser they're dealing with. This process is called *user agent sniffing* or, more broadly, device detection.

Sniffing up the wrong tree

Perhaps the most common criticism of user agent sniffing is that the information a browser provides isn't always reliable. Browsers, networks, and even users sometimes modify user agent information for myriad reasons, which makes it difficult to know if you're dealing with the browser you think you are. Let's start with a few popular mobile browsers' preference panels: Android's default browser, Opera Mini, the BlackBerry browser, and others provide an easy means of changing the name the browser reports itself as. You'll sometimes see this disguised as "Request desktop site" or with more granular settings like those in the Android browser, but the ability to change user agent information exists to give users the tools to fight against sites that deliver limited content and functionality to particular browsers (FIG 2.1).

Similarly, a browser's default user agent string is crowded with mentions of other browsers in hopes that they will prevent

FIG 2.1: Android, Opera, and Firefox user agent settings.

its users from being locked out of the best versions of certain sites. For example, in addition to several appropriate bits of information, the UA string of my current browser (Chrome 34) mentions Mozilla, Webkit, KHTML, Gecko, and Safari—all terms describing non-Chrome browsers:

```
Mozilla/5.0 (Macintosh; Intel Mac OS X 10_8_5)
AppleWebKit/537.36 (KHTML, like Gecko)
Chrome/34.0.1847.131 Safari/537.36
```

Some browsers go even further and deliberately obscure information in their user agent string to trick sites into sending them the experience other browsers get! The user agent string for the vastly improved Internet Explorer 11 never mentions Internet Explorer; instead, it tries to trick device-detection libraries into thinking the browser is Firefox or Webkit, which developers came to recognize as the only browsers that support advanced features necessary to deliver a better experience. (In recent versions of IE, this is thankfully no longer true.) In her *A List Apart* article "Testing Websites in Game Console Browsers," Anna Debenham notes a similar situation with the Sony PlayStation Vita's browser: "The Vita's browser is a WebKit-based version of NetFront. Strangely, it identifies itself as Silk in its user agent string, which is the browser for Amazon's Kindle Fire" (http://bkaprt.com/rrd/2-01/) (FIG 2.2).

Browser developers have an interest in ensuring the survival of their software. Ironically, the more web developers deliver their content and features unevenly based on user agent

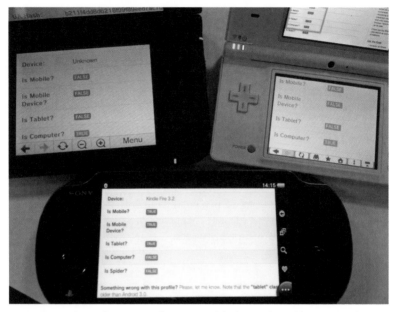

FIG 2.2: Messy device detection results across mobile devices (http://bkaprt.com/rrd/2-02/).

information, the less meaningful user agent information will continue to be.

"Set it and forget it?" Forget it!

But reliability is a minor problem compared to sustainability. We can only write detection logic against browsers and devices that exist now, which makes device detection utterly useless for gracefully accepting new browsers.

Most critically, relying too heavily on device detection can lead us to make dangerous assumptions based on information that's not always up to date. Device detection provides, at best, stock information about a device or browser, meaning any optimizations we make based on that static data may not reflect the live, dynamic nature of a user's actual browsing environment.

These are some examples of variables that a device database can never accurately convey (**FIG. 2.3**):

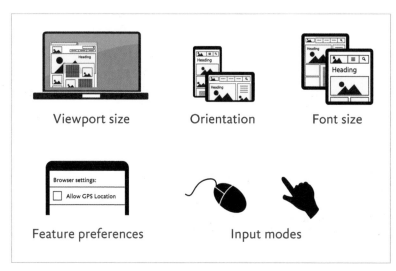

Viewport size   Orientation   Font size

Feature preferences   Input modes

FIG 2.3: Assumptions to avoid based on a device's user agent string.

- **Viewport size.** While a device database may return somewhat reliable information about a device's screen, screen size often differs from a browser's viewport size. For responsive layouts, it's the viewport size we care about. We should also avoid assuming anything about a user's connection speed based on screen size—smartphones are commonly used over fast Wi-Fi connections, while laptops and tablets can be tethered to a slow cell network—or worse: bus Wi-Fi.
- **Device orientation.** Those viewport considerations are twice as difficult when you consider display differences between portrait and landscape (**FIG 2.4**). Even if we know the dimensions of a screen, we have no way of knowing (on the server side) the device's orientation. We need to ship CSS that accommodates viewport variability.
- **Font size.** The common practice of using em-based units for media queries means that users' preferred default font size determines the layout they get, so a browser on a laptop with a large font size may need a smartphone-ish layout. (As we'll discuss in a bit, CSS media queries handle this naturally.)

FIG 2.4: The *Boston Globe* website shown in two screen orientations on the same device.

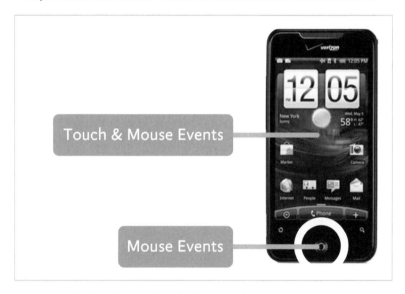

FIG 2.5: An Android 2.3 device with multiple input mechanisms.

- **Custom preferences.** People commonly override their browser defaults and turn off features on their phones. A browser may support a feature, but a server has no way of knowing whether that feature has been disabled by the user.
- **Input modes.** Device databases can often tell us if a device has a touch screen. But as you may recall, just because a device has a touch screen doesn't mean that it supports touch events, or that touch is the only input mechanism the device offers (**FIG 2.5**). And of course, touch support is now built into devices that have large screens as well, such as Google's Chromebook laptop, so it's unsafe to infer any sort of relationship between touch support and screen size.

So when we build cross-device experiences, we want to be mindful of these factors and be wary of assumptions based on stock device conditions. Device detection is a risky bet, and it's only going to get riskier.

GOOD NEWS: WE'RE IN CONTROL

The move away from browser-specific code has been long and slow, but support and tools for making sustainable, feature- and condition-based decisions have dramatically improved in recent years, and they get better every day. Client-side technology like HTML, CSS, and JavaScript allows us to see what's *actually* happening in that dynamic browser environment and to make decisions that are more contextual and appropriate. In a word: responsible.

Features and constraints, not devices

"An over-emphasis on context can focus design solutions too much on assumed mobile situations instead of on the true richness of mobile web use happening today."
—LUKE WROBLEWSKI, http://bkaprt.com/rrd/2-03/

One crutch we'd do well to abandon is the assumption that device form-factors are exclusively tied to specific browser features or network conditions. In reality, these features routinely overlap across common device categories.

"Touch and viewport size aren't connected. The most popular touch devices may currently be phones and tablets, but you can also find touch screen offerings for 27" monitors and beyond."
—TRENT WALTON, "Type & Touch" (http://bkaprt.com/rrd/2-04/)

Once-convenient mobile and desktop categories have lost any meaning for our work. We sometimes hear "mobile" to describe a device's roving physical context, yet vast amounts of smartphone and tablet use happen while people are at home on their couch. We may think of mobile as a connection-speed limitation, yet devices of all kinds are as likely to be tethered to high-speed Wi-Fi as they are to a high-latency cell tower (**FIG 2.6**). And we may take mobile to mean devices with features like a smaller screen size and an ability to react to touch, or constraints like poor rendering capabilities, but each day devices are released that break free from the neat categorizations we try to impose.

Attempting to classify devices and browsers by form factor alone distracts us from the parameters that are actually important when we design for the web: *features* (like CSS properties and JavaScript APIs) and *constraints* (like viewport size, unpredictable connectivity, or off-line use). Designing for features and constraints allows us to see how patterns that may otherwise seem distinct are shared across devices, and to build in a modular manner to create unique experiences that feel appropriate to each device.

Querying media responsibly

Perhaps the most memorable tenet from Ethan Marcotte's original responsive design workflow is CSS3 media queries, the conditional CSS statements we use to deliver styles to some contexts and not others. Marcotte's initial article used media queries in a desktop-first manner, which means that we build the largest layout first and use media queries to override that layout all the way down to a small screen.

Shifting the responsive direction

Toward the end of his book *Responsive Web Design,* Marcotte remarked that shifting our media queries to follow a mobile-first, or small-screen-first, philosophy would give our users a more responsible, sustainable experience. To paraphrase Luke Wroblewski, a mobile-first workflow helps us to prioritize content, since there's not enough room on a small screen for non-critical content. Thinking mobile-first also pairs nicely with the mindset of progressive enhancement, aka starting small and layering in more complex layout as space permits.

"The absence of support for @media queries is in fact the first @media query."
—BRYAN RIEGER, http://bkaprt.com/rrd/2-06/

A mobile-first responsive stylesheet begins with styles that are shared across all experiences, forming the foundation of the smallest screen layout. These styles are followed by a series of mostly `min-width` media queries to scale that layout up to greater viewport sizes and pixel depths. At a high level, the CSS looks something like this:

```
/* styles for small viewports here */
.logo {
  width: 50%;
  float: left;
}
.nav {
  width: 50%;
  float: right;
}

@media (min-width: 50em) {
  /* styles for viewport widths 50em and up here */
}

@media (min-width: 65em) {
  /* styles for viewports 65em and up here */
}
```

What about max?

When building mobile first, max-width queries are still quite
helpful. For example, if a design variation only occurs within a
certain width range, that's a great candidate for max-width. You
can combine min and max to isolate styles from CSS inheritance
at bigger breakpoints, making for smaller, simpler CSS:

```
@media (min-width: 50em) {
  .header {
    position: static;
  }
}

@media (min-width: 54em) and (max-width: 65em) {
  .header {
    position: relative;
  }
}
```

```
@media (min-width: 65em) {
  /* .header is static positioned here */
}
```

What's with those ems, anyway?

You may have noticed that in addition to shifting the responsive direction, the breakpoint widths above use em units rather than pixels. Ems are flexible units that are sized relative to an element's container in a layout. By using ems, we can design responsive breakpoints proportionally to our fluid, scalable content, which also tends to be designed with scalable units like em and %.

Converting pixel breakpoints to ems is easy: divide the pixel-based value by 16, the default equivalent size of 1em in most web browsers:

```
@media (min-width: 800px){
...
}
@media (min-width: 50em){  /* 800px / 16px */
...
}
```

If em breakpoints aren't your bag, pixels can work fine—I just prefer to use proportional units across a layout. The more important thing is to avoid basing breakpoints on device widths and instead focus on breakpoints that are appropriate to your site's content. For more information on em media queries, check out Lyza Gardner's article "The EMs have it: Proportional Media Queries FTW!" (http://bkaprt.com/rrd/2-07/).

Broadly qualifying CSS application

Not every mobile browser supports the CSS we rely on, like floats, positioning, or animation. If your styles for a small-screen experience are significantly complex, you might consider broadly qualifying their application to newer, media-query-supporting browsers. Wrapping the mobile-first styles in a media query such as `only all` is one reliable way to do this. Though a bit confusing to look at, the `only all` query applies in any browser that supports CSS3 media queries. While `all` is a CSS media type that refers to any browser that supports CSS 1.0, the `only` prefix requires media query support to understand—which means that its defined styles are recognized by modern browsers. Here's how our mobile-first stylesheet looks when qualified for media-query-supporting browsers:

```
@media only all {
  /* styles for qualified small viewports here */
}

@media (min-width: 50em) {
  /* styles for viewport widths 50em and up here */
}

@media (min-width: 65em) {
  /* styles for viewports 65em and up here */
}
```

Retaining some style in basic browsers

To maintain some level of branded experience in browsers that don't support media queries, I find it useful to tease out a small amount of the safer styles from your first CSS breakpoint and place them before the `only all` media query so they apply everywhere.

Safe styles—like `font-weight`, `margin`, `padding`, `border`, `line-height`, `text-align`, and more—can be sent to any browser without introducing problems (**FIG 2.7**).

```
/* styles for small viewports here */
body {
  font-family: sans-serif;
  margin: 0;
}
```

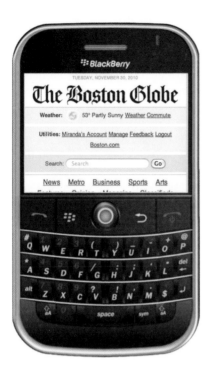

FIG 2.7: The basic experience of the *Boston Globe* website on an older BlackBerry.

```
a {
  font-color: #a00;
}
section {
  margin: 1em;
  border-bottom: 1px solid #aaa;
}

@media only all {
  /* styles for qualified small viewports here */
}
/* more... */
```

A quick (responsible) reminder: if you choose to deliver styles to basic browsers, be sure to test them!

Bullet-proofing the viewport

Traditionally (if such a term can be used for this stuff) in responsive layouts, we've used a `meta` element to specify the width that browsers should use to render a page when it first loads, such as the popular `width=device-width` declaration:

```
<meta name="viewport" content="width=device-width; »
    initial-scale=1">
```

This approach has worked fine for us so far, but it's not particularly sustainable: for starters, the W3C never standardized it; what's more, `meta` elements are a strange place to define a visual style. Thankfully, the W3C has standardized an approach to specifying viewport style information such as `width` and `scale`, and it's handled via CSS instead of HTML. To ensure that our viewport settings continue to work in future browser versions, we want to include these rules in our CSS:

```
@-webkit-viewport{width:device-width}
@-moz-viewport{width:device-width}
@-ms-viewport{width:device-width}
@-o-viewport{width:device-width}
@viewport{width:device-width}
```

For browsers that don't support `@viewport`, we should continue to include the `meta viewport` element. Trent Walton wrote a handy post about this, and includes tips for getting our responsive sites to work well with IE10's "snap mode" on Windows 8 (http://bkaprt.com/rrd/2-08/). (Unsurprising spoiler: getting things up to speed in IE10 requires more than the code above.)

Querying other media

Querying the width and height of a viewport with `min-width` and `max-width` goes a long way toward producing a usable layout, but there are many more conditions we can test to layer enhancements contextually. For instance, to deliver higher-dpi images to HD screens of 1.5× resolution and up, we can use a `min-resolution` media query of `144dpi` (twice that of standard `72dpi`). To cover some existing browsers currently transitioning to the standard syntax, we can also include a WebKit-prefixed fallback property (`-webkit-min-device-pixel-ratio`) in our query:

```
@media (-webkit-min-device-pixel-ratio: 1.5),
       (min-resolution: 144dpi) {
  /* Styles for HD screens here */
}
```

In the near future, media queries will support several more interesting features, such as detecting whether touch- or hover-based input mechanisms are supported via `@media (pointer:fine) {...}` and `@media (hover) {...}`, detecting JavaScript support via `@media (script){ ... }`, and even detecting ambient light with `luminosity`. To track their implementation status, keep an eye on Can I use... (http://bkaprt.com/rrd/2-09/), and for some great articles describing the "good and bad" of Level 4 media queries, see Stu Cox's article of that name (http://bkaprt.com/rrd/2-10/).

DETECTING FEATURES WITH JAVASCRIPT

As new features arrive in browsers, we often need to qualify their use at a more granular level. JavaScript feature detection has long been a part of web development, thanks to proprietary feature differences in early browsers. Back then and (to a lesser degree) to this day, to get code to work in more than one browser it was necessary to check whether even the most common functions were defined before using them. For example, if we wanted to listen for an event like `click`, we would first need to check which event API the browser supported:

```
// if standard event listeners are supported
if( document.addEventListener ){
  document.addEventListener( "click", myCallback, »
    false );
}
// if not, try the Internet Explorer attachEvent method
else if( document.attachEvent ){
  document.attachEvent( "onclick", myCallback );
}
```

Detecting JavaScript features

Thankfully, in recent years the web standards movement has nudged browsers into supporting common APIs for features like event handling, which greatly reduces the number of browser-specific forks we must apply in our code and makes it more sustainable in the long term.

Now it's more common to use JavaScript feature detection to determine whether a feature is supported, before using that feature to create enhancements on top of an already functional HTML experience. For example, the following JavaScript function detects whether the standard HTML canvas element (a sort of artboard element that offers an API for drawing graphics with JavaScript) is supported:

```
function canvasSupported() {
  var elem = document.createElement('canvas');
  return !!(elem.getContext && elem.getContext('2d'));
}
```

This could be used before loading and running a pile of canvas-dependent code:

```
if( canvasSupported() ){
  // use canvas API safely here!
}
```

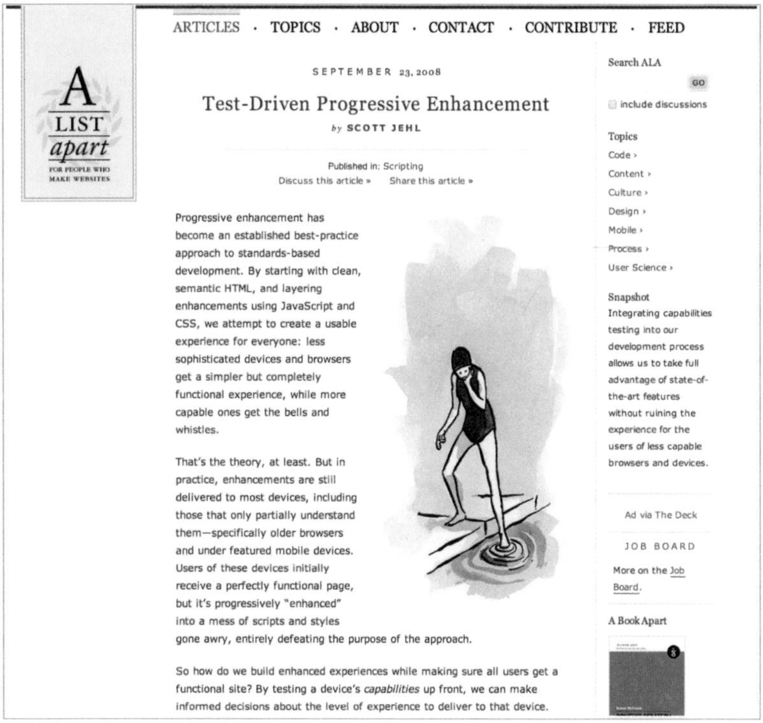
A LIST apart FOR PEOPLE WHO MAKE WEBSITES

ARTICLES · TOPICS · ABOUT · CONTACT · CONTRIBUTE · FEED

SEPTEMBER 23, 2008

Test-Driven Progressive Enhancement

by SCOTT JEHL

Published in: Scripting
Discuss this article » Share this article »

Progressive enhancement has become an established best-practice approach to standards-based development. By starting with clean, semantic HTML, and layering enhancements using JavaScript and CSS, we attempt to create a usable experience for everyone: less sophisticated devices and browsers get a simpler but completely functional experience, while more capable ones get the bells and whistles.

That's the theory, at least. But in practice, enhancements are still delivered to most devices, including those that only partially understand them—specifically older browsers and under featured mobile devices. Users of these devices initially receive a perfectly functional page, but it's progressively "enhanced" into a mess of scripts and styles gone awry, entirely defeating the purpose of the approach.

So how do we build enhanced experiences while making sure all users get a functional site? By testing a device's *capabilities* up front, we can make informed decisions about the level of experience to deliver to that device.

Search ALA
GO
include discussions

Topics
Code ›
Content ›
Culture ›
Design ›
Mobile ›
Process ›
User Science ›

Snapshot
Integrating capabilities testing into our development process allows us to take full advantage of state-of-the-art features without ruining the experience for the users of less capable browsers and devices.

Ad via The Deck

JOB BOARD
More on the Job Board.

A Book Apart

FIG 2.8: My 2008 *A List Apart* article "Test-Driven Progressive Enhancement" (http://bkaprt.com/rrd/2-11/).

Detecting CSS features

While detecting features in JavaScript isn't new, using JavaScript to detect CSS feature support began relatively recently. I first used CSS feature detection this way in the examples for my 2008 *A List Apart* article "Test-Driven Progressive Enhancement," which advocated the idea of running a series of diagnostic tests on a browser before applying CSS and JavaScript enhancements to a page (**FIG 2.8**).

At the time, new browsers included great new CSS capabilities like `float` and `position`, even though browsers with poor support for these features were widely used. This made it difficult to apply modern CSS to a site without breaking the experience for users running older browsers.

One example from the article was the following test to see if a browser *properly* supports the standard CSS box model, which incorporates `padding`, `width`, and `border` into the measured dimensions of an element. At the time, two different box model variations were actively supported across popular browsers, and writing CSS against one model would cause layouts to break in browsers (read: old versions of Internet Explorer) that supported the other.

```
function boxmodel(){
    var newDiv = document.createElement('div');
    document.body.appendChild(newDiv);
    newDiv.style.width = '20px';
    newDiv.style.padding = '10px';
    var divWidth = newDiv.offsetWidth;
    document.body.removeChild(newDiv);
    return divWidth === 40;
}
```

Let's look at this more closely. The JavaScript function creates a new `div` element, appends it to the `body` element in the document, and gives the `div` some `width` and `padding`. The function then returns a statement that the `div`'s rendered width should equal 40. Those familiar with the standard CSS box model will recall that the `width` and `padding` of an element contribute to its calculated width on the screen, so this function tells you whether the browser calculates that width as expected.

In the article, I bundled this test and others for properties like `float` or `position` into a suite called `enhance.js`, which could be run as a broad diagnostic during page load. If the test passed, the script would add a class of `enhanced` to the HTML element that could be used to qualify the application of advanced CSS properties.

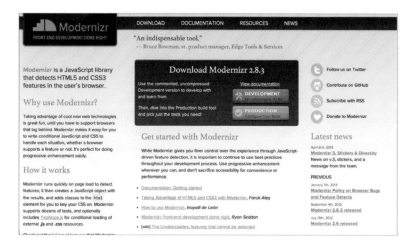

FIG 2.9: The Modernizr feature-testing framework.

```
.enhanced .main {
  float: left;
}
```

Qualifying CSS in this way felt like a sustainable step forward, but enhance.js was admittedly rough around the edges, since it couldn't detect and apply features at a granular level. Fortunately, developers much smarter than myself picked up the slack and took off running.

Feature detection frameworks

Almost any modern JavaScript framework uses feature tests within its internal codebase, but one framework stands alone in its mission to provide a standard approach to running tests in our sites: Modernizr (http://bkaprt.com/rrd/2-12/), created in 2009 by Paul Irish, Faruk Ateş, Alex Sexton, Ryan Seddon, and Alexander Farkas (FIG 2.9). Modernizr's simple workflow of adding specific classes to the html element to signify that a feature like CSS multi-columns is supported (<html class="...css-columns...">) makes the approach accessible to developers not versed in JavaScript detection intricacies, and has become a pseudo-standard approach to qualified application of enhancements.

Using Modernizr

Using Modernizr out of the box is quite straightforward. Include the `modernizr.js` script in the head of an HTML document, and the script runs feature tests automatically.

```
<script src="js/modernizr.js"></script>
```

When Modernizr tests run, the framework retains a JavaScript property, stored on the globally available `Modernizr` object, of that test's name that equals `true` if it passes or `false` if it doesn't.

```
if( Modernizr.canvas ){
  // Canvas is supported!
}
```

When a test passes, Modernizr also adds a class of that test's name to the `html` element, which you can then use within your CSS selectors to qualify the use of certain features. Quite a lot easier than hand-coding those tests above, right?

While you can safely use many modern CSS features without qualification—like `box-shadow`, `border-radius`, or `transition`—relying too heavily on these features can introduce usability issues in browsers that don't support them. For instance, say you want to overlay text on an image. You want a text color that matches the image and a text shadow to pull the characters forward (**FIG 2.10**).

```
.img-title {
  color: #abb8c7;
  text-shadow: .1em .1em .3em rgba( 0, 0, 0, .6 );
}
```

In browsers without `text-shadow` support, the text is nearly invisible (**FIG 2.11**)!

FIG 2.10: Our intended design.

FIG 2.11: Our design as viewed in a non-text-shadow-supporting browser.

To keep this from happening, you may choose to default to a different presentation, perhaps using a color with higher contrast first and then feature detection to enhance to the ideal presentation.

```
.img-title {
  color: #203e5b;
}
.textshadow .img-title {
  color: #abb8c7;
  text-shadow: .1em .1em .3em rgba( 0, 0, 0, .6 );
}
```

And voilà! You have yourself an accessible experience in browsers new *and* old (**FIG 2.12-2.13**).

FIG 2.12: Default experience.

FIG 2.13: Enhanced experience.

Detecting CSS support without JavaScript

As useful as JavaScript-driven feature detection is, it comes with the downside of loading and running code for no purpose other than to qualify features we want to use. Ideally, we should standardize the ways we detect features as we do the features themselves; thanks to advocacy from developer Paul Irish, native support for a CSS feature-detection approach has been standardized by the W3C and is gradually becoming available in browsers.

The @supports feature (http://bkaprt.com/rrd/2-13/) follows a similar syntax to that of media queries. By passing any CSS property and value pair (say, display: flex) to the @supports rule, you can define entire style blocks to apply only in browsers that implement that CSS feature (or features). Here's an example:

```
@supports ( display: flex ) {
  #content {
    display: flex;
  }
  ...more flexbox styles here
}
```

@supports is pretty handy: it offloads feature detection work to the browser, removing the need for us to write custom—and often slow, unreliable—tests to produce similar results. Less work for developers, and better performance for users! In addition to the @supports syntax in CSS, you can pair a JavaScript API called CSS.supports. Here's an example of it in action, qualifying the use of transition:

```
if( CSS.supports( "(transition: none)" ) ){
  // CSS transitions are supported!
  // Perhaps you'd add some transition event listeners
     here...
}
```

Support for support

As is the nature of many CSS features, the @supports approach to feature queries will gracefully degrade by itself, meaning you can safely include it in a stylesheet. Browsers that don't understand @supports will ignore it and the styles it qualifies.

We can't say the same of the JavaScript method that pairs with @supports: funnily enough, before using the CSS.supports JavaScript API, you need to check if the browser supports CSS.supports! If you've been developing websites for a while, you're probably used to this sort of thing. Somewhat amazingly, though, two versions of CSS.supports already exist in the wild because some versions of the Opera browser have a non-standard implementation (window.supportsCSS). So here's a snippet that tries to assign a variable cssSupports to one or the other, if available:

```
var cssSupports = window.CSS && window.CSS.supports || »
  window.supportsCSS;
```

With this normalization in place, you can qualify your `CSS.supports` use as follows:

```
if( cssSupports && cssSupports( "(transition: none)" »
  ) ){
  // CSS transitions are supported!
}
```

Now to play devil's advocate for a moment: one potential issue with native feature detection like `@supports` is that it places trust in browsers to report honest results about their own implementation's standards compliance. For example, the Android 2 browser supports `history.pushState`—used for changing the browser's URL location to reflect updates made in the page since last load—but it doesn't update the actual page address until you refresh the page, making the implementation completely useless. From a web developer's perspective, any variation from a W3C spec in a browser's implementation could deem a feature unusable, so where do we draw the line for whether a feature is supported or not? The spec suggests that support is defined by a browser implementing a particular property and value "with a usable level of support," which, of course, is subjective (http://bkaprt.com/rrd/2-14/). Given that in the past, browser vendors have routinely adjusted their user agent strings to improve their relevance among competitors, there's also the potential for deliberately dishonest reporting. As for how accurately this detection feature will continue to work, the future remains to be seen.

That leads us well into our next section.

UA detection: the best when all else fails

Sometimes, the question of whether a feature is supported is more complicated than a simple yes or no.

Uneven browser support is particularly problematic when it comes to talking about "the undetectables": features that are hard to detect across browsers through feature detection alone (http://bkaprt.com/rrd/2-15/). Scarily, a significant subset of these undetectables can wreak havoc on the usability or accessibility of content when they're unsupported or, often worse, partially supported. For example, Windows Phone 7 (running Internet Explorer 9) supports @font-face for delivering custom fonts, but only with fonts that are installed on the device—defeating the purpose of the feature.

Many features are partially or improperly supported in browsers. That presents a tedious challenge to responsible design: we have no way of knowing whether those features are working properly without testing the browser in question ourselves.

In situations where support for a technology you need is uneven and undetectable, and the lack of (or partial) support can create an undesirable effect, it may be a wise choice to employ some browser-based (rather than feature-based) detection as a fallback. It's worth noting, *yelling* even, that user agent detection has serious drawbacks and tends to be very unsustainable. Avoid it if you can. That said, it's sometimes necessary. The responsible approach is to do what we can to exhaust all potential means of browser-agnostic detection before resorting to the user agent string. Here are a couple of examples incorporating that last resort.

Desperately qualifying overflow

The CSS overflow property allows us to control what happens when content overflows the boundaries of an element. Possible values include visible (which visually displays the overflowed content), hidden (which hides it), and scroll or auto (which allows the user to scroll through the element's content). For example, the following CSS when applied to an element with a class of .my-scrolling-region:

```
.my-scrolling-region {
  border: 1px solid #000;
  height: 200px;
  width: 300px;
  overflow: auto;
}
```

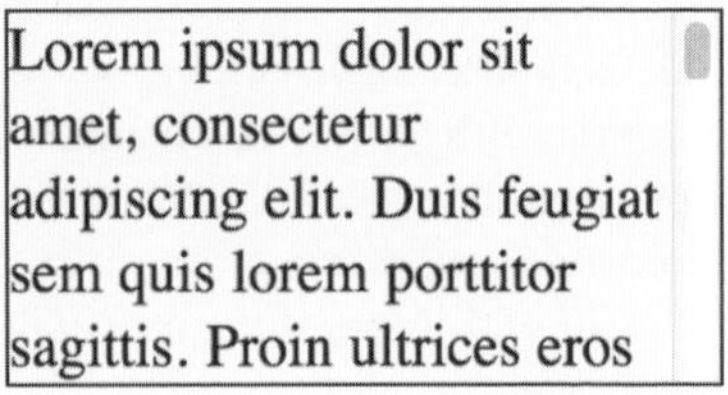

FIG 2.14: An example of the CSS overflow property.

...produces FIG 2.14 in the browser, if the content happens to exceed the height of the element.

Unfortunately, simple as it may sound, *partial* support for overflow is prevalent on the web. For example, many mobile browsers treat overflow: auto the same as overflow: hidden, which crops content without offering users any means of accessing it. What's more, older versions of iOS require two fingers to scroll an overflow region (which presumably few iOS users even know to try).

These support shortcomings make overflow risky to use without qualification, but to make matters worse, overflow support is nearly impossible to detect! A test for whether the overflow property is supported will pass even if it's not supported *properly*, and trying to test for overflow: auto support specifically requires user interaction to verify (i.e., we don't know for sure if scrolling works until the user tries it). Because of this predicament, overflow is a good candidate for a little user agent detection (as a fallback). Overthrow (http://bkaprt.com/rrd/2-16/) is a script that helps us use overflow safely; when the script runs, it takes the following steps:

It first runs a feature test to try to detect whether overflow is supported. This test will fail reliably in browsers that don't support overflow, and pass in most modern browsers that correctly support it. Unfortunately, though, the test also fails in several browsers that are known to support overflow properly, requiring a fallback approach to get those browsers on board. That approach checks the browser's user agent string to detect eight or so browsers that are known to render overflow properly yet fail the feature test. The script assumes those specific browsers will continue to support the feature in future versions as well (a slightly risky assumption). In passing browsers, Overthrow adds a class of `overthrow-enabled` to the HTML element, which can be used to qualify `overflow` within a stylesheet.

I want to reemphasize that we've attempted to use a browser-agnostic means of detecting the feature *before* resorting to device-specific logic. That part is critical, as we want to make our code as future-ready and sustainable as we can. With that class in place, we can qualify the element from above to safely use `overflow`:

```css
.overthrow-enabled .my-scrolling-region {
  overflow: auto;
  -webkit-overflow-scrolling: touch;
  -ms-overflow-style: auto;
  height: 200px;
}
```

The CSS shown here ensures that browsers that support `overflow` get a scrolling pane with a specific `height`, while others see the content in full without a set `height` that would require scrolling. Best of all, if the test malfunctions or fails to pass an `overflow`-supporting browser, the content will still be accessible. In addition to the `overflow` and `height`, I've added vendor-specific properties to apply momentum-based scrolling in WebKit and IE10 touch-based environments. **FIG 2.15** and **FIG 2.16** demonstrate supported versus unsupported environments—both perfectly usable.

Position: fixed? More like position: broken!

Another example of a dangerous undetectable is the CSS property `position:fixed`. Many recently popular mobile browsers (Android 2, Opera Mobile, older iOS versions) leave fixed-positioned content wherever it is at page load, meaning that content continues to sit on top of the content beneath it, obscuring access to the page (**FIG 2.17**).

FIG 2.15: The Overthrow site in a browser that supports overflow.

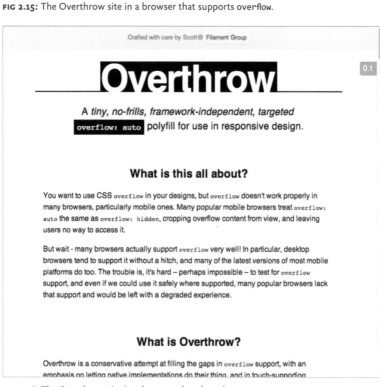

FIG 2.16: The Overthrow site in a browser that doesn't support overflow.

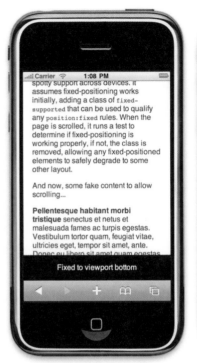
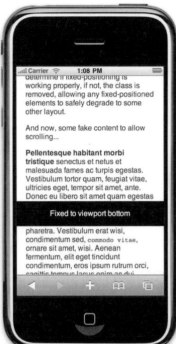

FIG 2.17: Intended behavior (left) vs. buggy behavior (right) in a browser with poor fixed-position support.

To combat this, check out Fixed-Fixed (http://bkaprt.com/rrd/2-17/). Similarly to Overthrow, Fixed-Fixed employs a simple CSS class qualifier you can use in your selectors; it also, like Overthrow, attempts to run a feature test before resorting to user-agent-based fallback detection if necessary. Here's an example:

```
.fixed-supported #header {
    position: fixed;
}
```

That's about it! In qualified browsers, the #header element is fixed to the top of the viewport; in others, it scrolls with the page.

Supporting the unsupported

If a browser doesn't support a particular feature, does that mean we have no way to use it in that browser? Not necessarily. In the past several years, the practice of emulating features in unsupported browsers, known as *shimming* or *polyfilling,* has become quite common. In fact, there's a workaround listed on the Modernizr site for almost every feature the library detects.

Shims tend to be quick hacks to enable a certain approach, while polyfills are more involved. Let's look at shims first.

Shims

Probably the most famous shim is the HTML5 shim, also called the HTML5 *shiv,* perhaps due to web developers' common disdain for older versions of Internet Explorer (more here: http://bkaprt.com/rrd/2-18/). IE versions older than 9 can't apply CSS styles to HTML elements that didn't exist at the time of the browser's release date, meaning HTML5 elements like section and header are unstyleable in one of the most widely used browsers on the web. Fortunately, a JavaScript workaround discovered by developer Sjoerd Visscher tricks IE into "learning" about any element that's generated with the method document.createElement, enabling IE to style those elements like any other. The workaround couldn't be easier: create an element of a given name using document.createElement, and all instances of that element IE subsequently encounters will be recognized as if natively supported, like magic.

Remy Sharp later created an open-source script (http://bkaprt.com/rrd/2-19/), now maintained by Alexander Farkas and others, that applies this workaround to the new HTML5 elements.

FIG 2.18: Unstyled, unrecognized HTML5 header element.

FIGURE 2.18 shows an example of HTML5 styling in IE8 without the shim.

```
<!DOCTYPE HTML>
<html>
<head>
  <style>
    header {
      font-size: 22px;
      color: green;
    }
  </style>
</head>
<body>
  <header>Website!</header>
</body>
</html>
```

FIG 2.19: Styled, shimmed HTML5 header element.

FIGURE 2.19 shows how it renders with the shim.

```
<!DOCTYPE HTML>
<html>
<head>
  <!--[if lt IE 9]>
  <script src="html5shiv.js"></script>
  <![endif]-->
  <style>
    header {
      font-size: 22px;
      color: green;
    }
  </style>
</head>
<body>
  <header>Website!</header>
</body>
</html>
```

With regard to responsible development, there is a minor but considerable downside to shimming HTML5 support: if the JavaScript fails to load in older IE browsers, HTML5 elements will not receive any CSS styles. This may not be a major problem if the only style we're applying is some color, as in the example above, but if a columnar page layout depends upon HTML5 element styling, the page elements will crash together in IE, which may hinder usability. To avoid this issue, it has become common to wrap HTML5 elements in a `div` with a class of that element name (`<div class="article"><article></article></div>`), and style that `div` element instead. This bloats the markup a little, but it does allow modern browsers to reap the semantic benefits of HTML5 elements without needing a JavaScript workaround to style the page.

Responsive design polyfills

The term *polyfill* was coined by Remy Sharp to describe an approach that Paul Irish sums up nicely as "a shim that mimics a future API providing fallback functionality to older browsers" (http://bkaprt.com/rrd/2-20/). A polyfill goes to some length to reproduce a standardized API with JavaScript, and is typically more than a quick-and-dirty workaround.

A responsible shim or polyfill should always try to discern if a feature is supported natively before reproducing its API. For performance reasons, a native implementation is always preferred, so it's also wise to consider whether the feature is truly necessary to polyfill in the first place. Nine times out of ten, it's more responsible to serve unsupported browsers a less-enhanced experience than to force ad hoc upgrades for features they don't support. The decision to use a polyfill should be based on three main points: how much the feature improves your audience's user experience, the cost to performance of including the polyfill in a page, and its ability to one day be removed seamlessly from your codebase.

For responsive design, I commonly find a few polyfills helpful.

MatchMedia: media queries in JavaScript

While media queries are mostly used for applying CSS, sometimes it's useful to know whether a media query applies to JavaScript logic as well. One example may be when requesting additional, appropriately sized images for a gallery. MatchMedia enables us to evaluate media queries in JavaScript.

To use it, simply pass any media type or query to the window. matchMedia function, and it will return an object with a matches property that is either true or false depending on whether the media applies at that time:

```
if( window.matchMedia( "(min-width: 45em)" ).matches ){
  // The viewport is at least 45em wide!
}
```

Okay, I didn't mention a slight wrinkle: matchMedia is not supported in every browser that supports CSS3 media queries. So, before using it we either need to check to see if it's supported at all or use a polyfill to make it work where it otherwise wouldn't. For those interested in the latter option, I wrote a polyfill for matchMedia a few years back, and Paul Irish was kind enough to set up a GitHub repository where we've continued to maintain the script (FIG 2.20).

To use the polyfill, simply reference the matchMedia.js file in your page to use window.matchMedia in any browser, even one that doesn't support CSS media queries! Not so fast, though: you still need to be in a media-query-supporting browser for any media query value to match (though media types like screen work in just about any device with a screen).

With the polyfill in place, you can now use matchMedia to test whether CSS3 media queries are natively supported, which could be useful if you want to qualify the addition of advanced scripting that should only apply in modern browsers. Just like in CSS itself, the only all media query can give us just that information.

FIG 2.20: The `matchMedia.js` Project by Scott Jehl, Paul Irish, and Nicholas Zakas (http://bkaprt.com/rrd/2-21/).

```
if( window.matchMedia( "only all" ).matches ){
  // Media queries are natively supported!
}
```

Another potentially useful feature of the `matchMedia` API is its ability to accept *listeners,* allowing us to keep an ear out for changes to a particular `matchMedia` query's state after we check it the first time. To ensure it'll work broadly, the `matchMedia.js` polyfill has a listener extension to support this part of the API as well. Adding a `matchMedia` listener is pretty straightforward: call a `matchMedia` function as seen above and assign an `addListener` method to the end of it, like this:

```
window.matchMedia( "(min-width: 45em)" ).addListener( »
  callback );
```

In this case, `callback` is a function you can define that executes every time the media query changes its state between `true` and `false`. The first argument passed to the `callback` function contains a reference to the `matchMedia` object, allowing easy access to its `matches` property whenever the listener fires. Here's an example of how that function can plug in:

```
window.matchMedia( "(min-width: 45em)" )
  .addListener( function( mm ){
    if( mm.matches ){
      // The viewport is at least 45em in width!
    }
    else {
      // The viewport is less than 45em in width!
    }
} );
```

Media queries to IE: please respond, IE.

As you'll likely remember from earlier in this chapter, Internet Explorer versions 8 and older don't support CSS media queries. This means that a mobile-first responsive layout will render in a layout intended for small screens on a desktop computer—still usable, but not formatted in an ideal way for large-screen use (**FIG 2.21**).

This drawback might put a damper on the whole responsive design thing if it weren't for some reliable workarounds.

First, we have a small polyfill script, `respond.js` (http://bkaprt.com/rrd/2-22/), that I developed during the *Boston Globe* project to make old IE versions render responsive layouts as if they understood CSS3 media queries. `respond.js` works by reading every stylesheet referenced in a document to find all the media queries contained therein. The script parses the values of these media queries to look for either a minimum or maximum width that can be compared against the viewport window's dimensions. When it finds a query that matches, it injects the styles contained in that query into a style block in the page, allowing the styles to apply in browsers that do not understand media queries, and the script reruns this logic whenever the

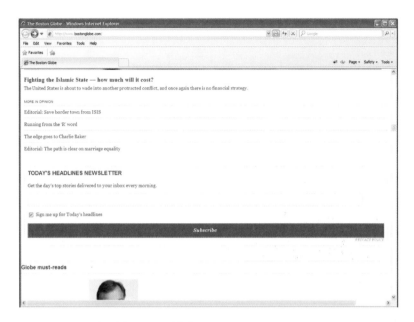

FIG 2.21: An example of the *Boston Globe* homepage in IE8.

browser is resized (and when a device's orientation changes). `respond.js` is intentionally limited in scope to keep it small and fast, so it only supports `min-width` and `max-width` media queries, which should be enough to pull off a reasonably responsive layout for users of old IE.

To use `respond.js`, reference the script in your page anywhere after your CSS references. I recommend using an IE conditional comment (a special comment syntax that old IE browsers are designed to ignore) around the script tag as well, so that the file is only requested in the versions of Internet Explorer that need it. This particular conditional comment says: "If the browser is IE less than version 9, parse the content of this comment like all other HTML on the page."

```
<!--[if lt IE 9]><script src="respond.js"> »
  </script><![endif]-->
```

FIG 2.22: *The Boston Globe* website, viewed in IE8 with respond.js used for media query support.

By including this script, the *Boston Globe* homepage is more usable in old IE (**FIG 2.22**).

Avoiding the polyfill with static CSS

Another responsible approach to addressing old IE's lack of media query support is to serve IE additional CSS rules that essentially force it into rendering the styles from a responsive design's wider breakpoints. You can do this manually or with the help of CSS preprocessors such as Sass. For more on this approach, check out Jeremy Keith's 2013 article "Dealing with IE" (http://bkaprt.com/rrd/2-23/).

This approach is only able to serve users running old IE a fluid, but not responsive, layout, which may be fine depending on how broadly your fluid layout scales. However, depending on your user's screen size and your particular layout, it may or may not make for an ideal experience.

Avoiding doing anything at all

As a third option, you might simply do nothing at all and serve the responsive site to old IE as is. This leaves the layout in its default non-media-query state. Depending on the layout, this can be perfectly fine, especially if you set a reasonable `max-width` on the layout to keep the line lengths in check.

TESTING RESPONSIBLY

To ensure that a site works across a variety of screen sizes, input types, and browsers, you can't beat testing on real devices. To get a decent idea of the devices that it would make sense to amass for a personal testing lab, see Brad Frost's excellent post "Test on Real Mobile Devices without Breaking the Bank" (http:// bkaprt.com/rrd/2-24/).

Devices are expensive to collect, so to test on an array of relevant devices, the average developer may need to search for a nearby community device lab, which is thankfully becoming more common (**FIG 2.23**). For information about device labs in your area, visit Open Device Lab (http://bkaprt.com/rrd/2-25/).

Testing on real devices is ideal, but we can't possibly expect to have access to even a fraction of the devices we need to care about. When you don't have access to a device, a device emulator is a brilliant solution. Emulated devices do come with drawbacks, such as misleading performance (because the browser is running on different hardware than it would normally run on), slow screen refresh rates that make animation difficult to test, connection speeds that are often faster than the device would typically have, and a lack of physical feedback that allows us to get a true sense for how a site feels on a particular device. But despite the downsides, emulators are a very reliable means of diagnosing issues with CSS layout and JavaScript.

These days I do most of my own emulated browser testing on BrowserStack (http://bkaprt.com/rrd/2-27/), which offers real-time browser testing on platforms like iOS, Android, and

FIG 2.23: Friends gathered around a collection of test devices and laptops. Photograph by Luke Wroblewski (http://bkaprt.com/rrd/2-26/).

Opera Mobile, as well as various Windows and Mac desktop browsers (FIG 2.24). BrowserStack even offers a way to easily test local sites on your machine, so you don't need to upload anything to test a page.

Also, I spend the vast majority of my development time in a browser with strong developer tools, like Google Chrome or Firefox, as their code inspectors give incredibly helpful insights into how a site's various components are working in unison, and even allow me to test features that aren't enabled in the browser by default, like touch events. I only branch out to other physical and emulated devices once a feature works to verify usability and performance, a process I repeat over and over throughout the development cycle.

As the number of web-accessing devices has grown, browser testing has become a nuanced activity, requiring developers to make subjective decisions about minor variations in the experience that individual devices receive. When pulling up a site on a

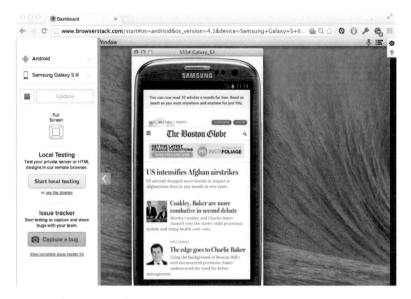

FIG 2.24: The Browserstack testing service.

particular device, I like to ask myself a series of questions about the site's design and functionality:

- Does the site load and present itself in a reasonable amount of time?
- Is the core content and functionality usable and accessible?
- Does the level of enhancement in the layout feel appropriate to the device?
- Is the text easy to scan? Do the line lengths promote readability?
- Is the site controllable and browsable via common input mechanisms on the device (touch, mouse, keyboard, etc.)?
- Are the actionable areas of the page easy to tap without tapping on adjacent items?
- Does the layout hold up to changes in orientation, viewport resizing, and font size?

- If the device has assistive technology installed (such as VoiceOver), does the content read back in meaningful ways?
- Does the page scroll efficiently? Do animations run smoothly?

The more devices we can test, the better our chances of reaching our users wherever they are.

NEXT UP

In this chapter, we covered many of the complexities of writing sustainable, cross-browser code. With that, we can proceed to our fourth tenet of responsible responsive design: performance. Because performance is a heavy topic—perhaps the one most in need of our attention when building responsive websites today—I've dedicated two chapters to its discussion.

Let's move ahead—with speed.

3 PLANNING FOR PERFORMANCE

WE'RE NOT DOING A GOOD JOB

Page-load times in the ten-second range are still common on modern mobile networks, and that's a fraction of how long it takes in countries with older, more limited networks. Why so slow? It's mostly our fault: our sites are too heavy, and they're often assembled and delivered in ways that don't take advantage of how browsers work. According to HTTP Archive (http://bkaprt. com/rrd/3-02/), the average website weighs 1.7 megabytes. (It's probably heftier now, so you may want to look it up.) To make matters worse, most of the sites surveyed on HTTP Archive aren't even responsive, but focus on one specific use case: the classic desktop computer with a large screen.

That's awful news for responsive (and, ahem, *responsible*) designers who aim to support many types of devices with a single codebase, rather than focusing on one type. Truth be told, much of the flak responsive design has taken relates to the ballooning file sizes of responsive sites in the wild, like Oakley's admittedly gorgeous Airbrake MX site (http://bkaprt.com/rrd/3-03/), which originally launched with a whopping 80-megabyte file size (though it was later heavily optimized to be much more responsible), or the media-rich Disney homepage, which serves a 5-megabyte responsive site to any device.

Why are some responsive sites so big? Attempting to support every browser and device with a single codebase certainly can have an additive effect on file size—if we don't take measures to prevent it. Responsive design's very nature involves delivering code that's ready to respond to conditions that may or may not occur, and delivering code only when and where it's needed poses some tricky obstacles given our current tool set.

Fear not!

Responsible responsive designs are achievable even for the most complex and content-heavy sites, but they don't happen on their own. Delivering fast responsive sites requires a deliberate focus on our delivery systems, because how we serve and apply our assets has an enormous impact on perceived and actual page-loading performance. In fact, how we *deliver* code matters more than how much our code weighs.

Delivering responsibly is hard, so this chapter will take a deep, practical dive into optimizing responsive assets for eventual delivery over the network. First, though, we'll tour the anatomy of the loading and enhancement process to see how client-side code is requested, loaded, and rendered, and where performance and usability bottlenecks tend to happen.

Ready? Let's take a quick look at the page-loading process.

A WALK DOWN THE CRITICAL PATH

Understanding how browsers request and load page assets goes a long way in helping us to make responsible decisions about

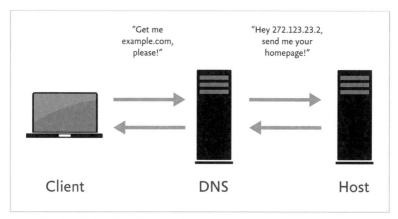

"Get me
example.com,
please!"

"Hey 272.123.23.2,
send me your
homepage!"

Client   DNS   Host

FIG 3.1: The foundation of a web connection.

how we deliver code and speed up load times for our users. If you were to record the events that take place from the moment a page is requested to the moment that page is usable, you would have what's known in the web performance community as the *critical path*. It's our job as web developers to shorten that path as much as we can.

A simplified anatomy of a request

To kick off our tour de HTTP, let's start with the foundation of everything that happens on the web: the exchange of data between a browser and a web server. Between the time when our user hits go and their site begins to load, an initial request pings back and forth from their browser to a local *Domain Name Service* (which translates the URL into an IP address used to find the host), or DNS, to the host server (**FIG 3.1**).

That's the basic rundown for devices accessing the web over Wi-Fi (or an old-fashioned Ethernet cable). A device connected to a mobile network takes an extra step: the browser first sends the request to a local cell tower, which forwards the request to the DNS to start the browser-server loop. Even on a popular connection speed like 3G, that radio connection takes ages in computer terms. As a result, establishing a mobile connection

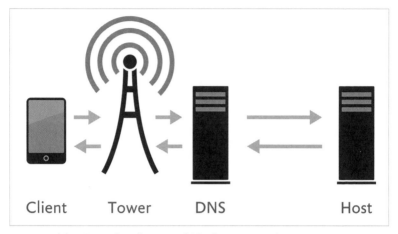

Client   Tower   DNS   Host

FIG 3.2: Mobile? First to the cell tower! Which takes two seconds on average over 3G (http://bkaprt.com/rrd/3-04/).

to a remote server can lag behind Wi-Fi by two whole seconds or more (FIG 3.2).

Two seconds may not seem like a long time, but consider that users can spot—and are bothered by—performance delays as short as 300 milliseconds. That crucial two-second delay means the mobile web is inherently slower than its Wi-Fi counterpart.

Thankfully, modern LTE and 4G connections alleviate this pain dramatically, and they're slowly growing in popularity throughout the world. We can't rely on a connection to be fast, though, so it's best to assume it won't be. In either case, once a connection to the server is established, the requests for files can flow without tower connection delays.

REQUESTS, REQUESTS, REQUESTS!

Say our browser requests an HTML file. As the browser receives chunks of that HTML file's text from the server, it parses them procedurally, looking for references to external assets that must also be requested, and converts the HTML into a tree structure of HTML elements known as a *Document Object Model*, or DOM. Once that DOM structure is built, JavaScript methods can traverse and manipulate the elements in the document pro-grammatically and CSS can visually style the elements however we like.

The complexities of HTML parsing (and its variations across browsers) could fill a book. Lest it be ours, I will be brief: the important thing is getting a grasp on the fundamental order of operations when a browser parses and renders HTML.

- CSS, for example, works best when all styles relevant to the initial page layout are loaded and parsed *before* an HTML document is rendered visually on a screen.
- In contrast, JavaScript behavior is often able to be applied to page elements *after* they're loaded and rendered.

But both JavaScript and CSS present bumps on the critical path, blocking our page from showing while they load and ex-ecute. Let's dig into this order of operations a bit.

Rendering and blocking

The quickest-to-load HTML document is one without extra ex-ternal files, but it's also not one you'll commonly find. A typical HTML document references a slew of outside assets like CSS, JavaScript, fonts, and images.

You can often spot CSS and JavaScript in the HTML docu-ment's head as link and script elements, respectively. By de-fault, browsers wait to render a page's content until these assets finish loading and parsing, a behavior known as *blocking* (FIG 3.3). By contrast, images are a non-blocking asset, as the browser won't wait for an image to load before rendering a page.

Despite its name, blocking rendering for CSS does help the user interface load consistently. If you load a page before its CSS is available, you'll see an unstyled default page; when the CSS finishes loading and the browser applies it, the page content will reflow into the newly styled layout. This two-step process is called a *flash of unstyled content*, or FOUC, and it can be ex-tremely jarring to users. So blocking page rendering until the CSS is ready is certainly desirable as long as the CSS loads in a short period of time—which isn't always an easy goal to meet.

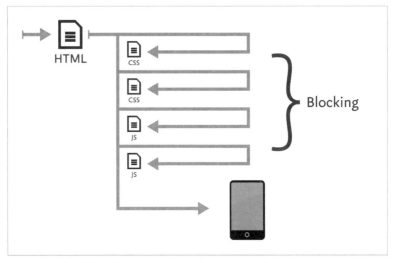

FIG 3.3: Blocking CSS and JavaScript requests during page load.

Blocking's value with regard to JavaScript almost always undermines the user experience and is more a response to a lingering JavaScript method called document.write, used to inject HTML directly into the page at whatever location the browser happens to be parsing. It's usually considered bad practice to use document.write now that better, more decoupled methods are available in JS, but document.write is still in use, particularly by scripts that embed advertisements. The biggest problem with document.write is that if it runs after a page finishes loading, it overwrites the entire document with the content it outputs. More like document.wrong, am I right? (I'm so sorry.) Unfortunately, a browser has no way of knowing whether a script it's requesting contains a call to document.write, so the browser tends to play it safe and assume that it does. While blocking prevents a potential screen wipe, it also forces users to wait for scripts before they can access the page, even if the scripts wouldn't have caused problems. Avoiding use of document.write is one important step we can take to address this issue in JavaScript. In the next chapter, we'll cover ways to load

FIG 3.4: The Network pane in Chrome.

scripts that avoid this default blocking behavior and improve perceived performance as a result.

GET COMFY WITH YOUR DEVELOPER TOOLS

Our browsers come with incredible built-in tools to help us inspect, test, and analyze our pages to see exactly what's happening under the hood. It's worthwhile to familiarize yourself with these tools in several browsers, but I'll cover my personal favorite, the developer tools panel from Chrome. When it comes to page-load performance, two panes are especially useful: Network and Timeline.

The Network pane is your window into the details of all the assets the browser requests to render the page (FIG 3.4). It has columns for file type, cache status, size, and request time, among others, and at the bottom of the panel you'll find a tally of the totals. My friend Mat Marquis likes to call this the "judgement pane," and I agree: it's the best way to evaluate the details of a website's delivery.

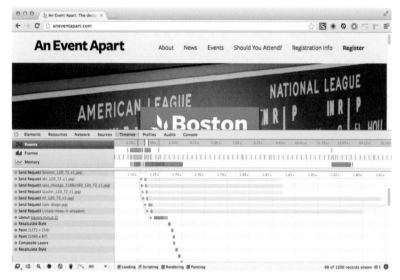

FIG 3.5: The Chrome developer tools' Timeline pane.

The Timeline pane gives us a deep look into the order in which assets load and render, and presents these events in a handy waterfall-style chart that you can scan from top to bottom, left to right, along a time axis (**FIG 3.5**). With the Timeline panel, we can record the page-loading process or a user-interaction sequence, and investigate how long it took to render parts of a page, which HTTP requests blocked that rendering from happening sooner, and if any of our enhancements caused the browser to reflow (adjust the position of elements on the page) or repaint (re-render an element in place) content. Using this tool, I often discover tweaks I can make to how my files are concatenated and loaded, and then I can record again to test whether my changes improved performance.

Browsers act differently when loading and parsing assets, so I recommend getting comfortable working in more than one browser's developer tools. IE, Firefox, Opera, Safari, and mobile browsers like Chrome for Android and iOS Safari all have debugging capabilities that are easy to use and incredibly helpful when scouting out bugs. For help using the developer tools in your browser of choice, visit Secrets of the Browser Developer Tools (http://bkaprt.com/rrd/3-05/).

Perceived performance: your most critical metric

It's important to think of performance in terms of both quantitative measured time and weight and how a page load is perceived. After all, a page is often usable long before every asset has finished downloading; that perceived load time is often more important to us than the total page-load time (it may take ten seconds for a page to fully load over 3G, but the user can interact with the page after only a few seconds or less). While we have ways to improve perceived performance without actually improving page load time (like displaying a loading icon while other content finishes loading), there are widely agreed-upon goals for what constitutes a page-load time that is "fast enough." Among the performance community, the one-second page load has emerged as a de facto standard goal, and great resources exist to explain the optimizations that help you get there.

One such resource is Google's PageSpeed Insights (http://bkaprt.com/rrd/3-06/). PageSpeed Insights offers a web application and browser extensions for analyzing your sites and recommending improvements. Here's a screencap of how Filament Group's highly optimized site fares in PageSpeed's tests (**FIG 3.6**). For the record, it's entirely acceptable to brag about how fast your site loads!

To test how your site is doing in terms of perceived performance, I highly recommend the tools at WebPagetest (http://bkaprt.com/rrd/3-07/), a project developed by Patrick Meenan at Google (**FIG 3.7**). To use WebPagetest, enter a URL and fill out the various form fields for the results you want to see—you can even choose to test from different locations around the world, which can be eye-opening. Once the test runs, you'll get detailed results about page performance data.

Out of all of WebPagetest's metrics, Speed Index is perhaps the most relevant for keeping tabs on perceived performance. The Speed Index formula considers factors like viewport size and the time at which the page starts rendering (which translates into a score that represents the time a page takes to first become

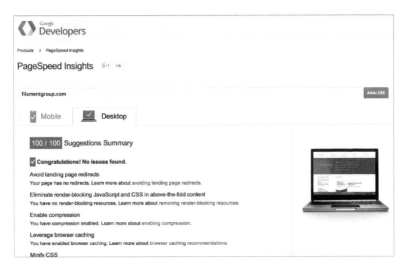

FIG 3.6: PageSpeed Insights test results for the Filament Group site.

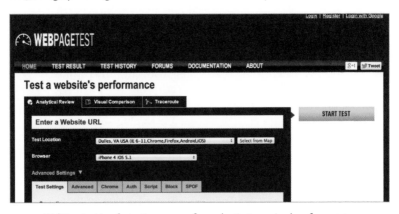

FIG 3.7: WebPagetest is a fantastic resource for evaluating perceived performance.

usable); the lower the score, the better. Per Google, the average Speed Index for an Alexa top-300,000 site is 4493, while a top-ten percentile score is 1388. How fast is fast enough? Google developer Paul Irish says that 1000 is a great score to shoot for (http://bkaprt.com/rrd/3-08/).

Getting a low Speed Index isn't easy, and even once we have things in a good place, all it takes is a scope change—say, the addition of third-party advertising or an off-the-shelf slideshow component—to ruin the perceived performance of a well-optimized site. To combat these situations, I find that it helps to suggest establishing a performance budget as early as possible.

INTRODUCING A PERFORMANCE BUDGET

The idea of a performance budget is fairly new, and it seems that the web community is still tinkering with how to define such a budget, let alone enforce it. That said, the basic idea is sound: a performance budget is a number, or set of numbers, used as a guideline for whether you can afford a particular code addition to a codebase, or whether an existing site's performance needs to improve. These numbers can represent page transfer weight ("page should weigh no more than X kilobytes and make no more than Y requests"), or perceived load time ("page should be usable in X seconds or less"), though I prefer to keep an eye on both. I also find that getting your client excited about these numbers is helpful in maintaining them throughout the development process; the numbers aren't just for the technical team—everyone should be kept up-to-date.

On that note, I should point out that performance is not merely a technical concern, but also often a cultural one within organizations. Good performance is good design, and performance should be a priority from the start rather than an afterthought saved for developers to handle. Decisions made in a project's early stages have an enormous effect on the constraints we face when we move to code, and developers should assert themselves early in the site-planning process to keep team members aware of how their content and design strategies affect a site's performance. As Tim Kadlec points out in his post "Holistic Performance": "Performance is not just a developmental concern, it's a fundamental component of the user experience" (http://bkaprt.com/rrd/3-09/).

Figuring out what the numbers in a performance budget should be is difficult, and it varies across projects. If you're starting fresh, an analysis of the performance of your competitors' sites can give you a good idea of the budget you want to work against and what times you want to beat. Focus on the enhancements you're adding to your site and try to limit how much extra stuff you deliver to keep that timing in check.

Lately, I've enjoyed using Tim Kadlec's Grunt-PerfBudget tool (http://bkaprt.com/rrd/3-10/) for keeping tabs on our performance budget as we continue to develop a codebase. Kadlec's tool is a command-line utility that you can automate to run whenever you make changes to your site. By default, the tool tests your pages on remote WebPagetest servers and reports back whether you are passing or failing the budget you've set. I tend to keep our budget at 1000 (one second) for Speed Index for Initial Render. Here's how the tool reports back when I run it:

```
$ grunt perfbudget
Running "perfbudget:dev" (perfbudget) task
Running test...
Test ID ADKLKJCLKD.... obtained....
Test Pending...
Test Started...
>> --------------------------------------------
>> Test for http://client-website.com/     FAILED
>> --------------------------------------------
>> render: 594 [PASS]. Budget is 1000
>> SpeedIndex: 1049 [FAIL]. Budget is 1000
>> Summary: http://www.webpagetest.org/result/140712_
EJ_....
```

REQUESTING LESS

If I could give only one piece of advice about requests, it would be to reduce the number of blocking requests you make in your document. Every blocking HTTP request is a barrier between our users and the content they seek. If a blocking request fails to load, a user is locked out of your site until that request expires, which can last up to thirty seconds in today's most-used browsers. That's a lot of time for your users to stare at a charming white timed-out screen—assuming they haven't already left.

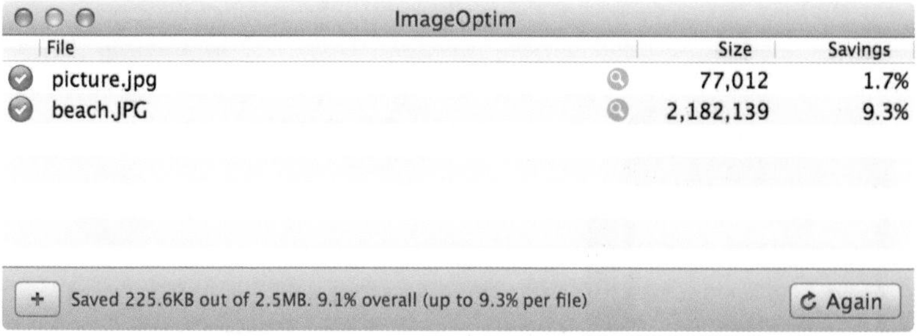

FIG 3.8: The drag-and-drop ImageOptim interface.

After we cut down our blocking requests, we can do much more to optimize the files we're delivering to make them load faster.

PREPARING FILES FOR WEB DELIVERY

When preparing front-end files for delivery, it's important to both reduce the total number of files you send over the network and make those files as small as possible.

Optimize image files

To make sure the images we deliver are as light as they can be, it's critical to optimize their compression. Compressing an image can be as simple as tweaking the export settings in Photoshop's Save for Web panel, but we have other tools designed purely for image optimization. My go-to for ease of use is ImageOptim (http://bkaprt.com/rrd/3-11/), which has a simple drag-and-drop interface for batch-processing images (FIG 3.8). Drop images over the window, and they'll be overwritten with optimized versions.

If you want to automate such optimization, try some of the powerful command-line image-compression tools available. OptiPNG (http://bkaprt.com/rrd/3-12/) and jpegtran (http://bkaprt.com/rrd/3-13/) are designed to optimize PNG and JPEG images, respectively, and are easy to hook into an automated build workflow via tools like grunt-contrib-imagemin (http://bkaprt.com/rrd/3-14/).

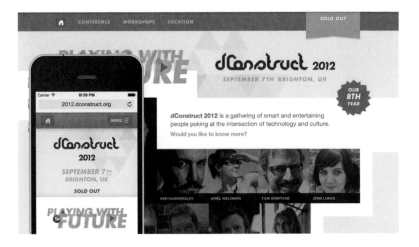

FIG 3.9: The responsibly built dConstruct Conference site (http://bkaprt.com/rrd/3-15/).

When it comes to optimizing images, simpler graphics tend to compress better than those with many colors and gradients. Some designers have even gone so far as to let file size constraints lead them to creative visual solutions they might not have explored otherwise. For example, the dConstruct 2012 site built by the amazing team at Clearleft featured duotone imagery designed to cut image weight while looking unique and compelling (FIG 3.9). Despite its rich visuals, the entire homepage weighs only 230 kilobytes!

Concatenate text files

Reducing the number of loaded files doesn't necessarily mean deleting them; the practice of automatically combining files, or *concatenation*, is common with CSS and JavaScript. After all, the fewer blocking requests, the better. You can concatenate files by hand or automate the process, though for any sufficiently complex site I recommend letting tools do the work.

```
jquery-2.1.0.min.js    ●
1    /*! jQuery v2.1.0 | (c) 2005, 2014 jQuery Foundation, Inc. | jquery.org/lic
2    !function(a,b){"object"==typeof module&&"object"==typeof module.expc
3    while(c--)d=g[c].name,0===d.indexOf("data-")&&(d=o.camelCase(d.slic
4    return d||(f=$b[b],$b[b]=e,e=null!=c(a,b,d)?b.toLowerCase():null,$b[b]=f
5
```

FIG 3.10: A minified copy of jQuery viewed in Sublime Text 2.

One quick example of this is the $ cat command run within a Terminal window, which accepts any number of space-separated file paths followed by a > character to specify a new file comprised of the combined contents of the listed files:

```
$ cat foo.js bar.js > foobar.js
```

Minify text files

Once we've reduced the number of files that will load for any given device, we want to make those concatenated files as small as possible. We have a couple ways to do so. The first is called *minification*, which is the practice of automatically removing any portions of the file that aren't needed when a browser parses the file. In HTML files, those portions mostly refer to white space and line breaks between HTML elements. In CSS and JavaScript files, the portions typically include white space, comments, and line breaks, but JavaScript minification often goes further, using techniques like renaming variables to use fewer characters (since the variable names themselves don't need to make sense to a computer) (FIG 3.10).

Often, the source of a minified file ends up as a single line of text without any line breaks.

On a site like jQuery's download page, minified files are often called *production versions* due to their lack of human readability and line numbers that help during debugging. (A lack of line breaks means a lack of line numbers!)

Compress text files

Once our text files are concatenated and minified, we want to ascertain that they're compressed before we send them across the web. A common compression protocol, Gzip, makes text files smaller for transfer between server and browser. For more on how Gzip and its Deflate algorithm work, check out Antaeus Feldspar's explanation (http://bkaprt.com/rrd/3-16/).

With each request, all modern browsers are configured to notify a server that they're able to decompress Gzip-compressed files, and Gzip is easy to configure on most any web server. For example, to enable Gzip for all HTML, CSS, and JavaScript files on an Apache server, add a file called .htaccess to your website's public root folder and make sure it contains these instructions:

```
<IfModule mod_deflate.c>
AddOutputFilterByType DEFLATE text/html text/css text/
javascript
</IfModule>
```

To check whether Gzip is functioning, load your site and open your browser's developer tools' Network panel. If you see two file sizes listed for a given file, you're set. For example, in Chrome's panel, you can check the Size column to see a small and a large size (3.7 kb and 7.6 kb, as shown in FIG 3.11). Those represent a file's transfer size (with Gzip) and actual size (after decompression in the browser), respectively.

Cache rules everything around us

A discussion on preparing assets for delivery would be incomplete without mentioning a browser's caching behaviors—the process of storing a static, local copy of a file. Caching is a complex topic, but a basic understanding of how it works and the various caches we access in modern browsers helps a great deal in speeding up our sites.

FIG 3.11: An example of a Gzip-compressed JavaScript request in Chrome's developer tools.

Optimize for typical caching

The first cache to consider is the browser's default cache. The default cache's job is to automatically store any files it requests so that the next time those files are requested, it can avoid a network request and instead use the local copy. On a given website, most of the assets we serve can afford to be cached for a short time in the browser, and many can be cached for a very long duration. An exception to this rule is highly dynamic content, like the text in a live-text chat feed.

When you serve files on the web, you're able to configure the ways in which any given file should be cached. This is done by setting response headers, which are simply metadata that the server includes with each response. Response headers are simple to configure with any web server, such as Apache. For example, setting the Expires header to a far-future date like a month or a year from the time it's served instructs the browser to keep it until then. Be careful, though, as you only want longer-term caching for files that aren't apt to change anytime soon (like CSS, JavaScript, images, and font files—but probably not the HTML for a list of recent articles). For great information on configuring your files for optimal caching, see HTML5 Boilerplate's recommendations (http://bkaprt.com/rrd/3-17/) and also Google's Make the Web Faster suite of tools (http://bkaprt.com/rrd/3-18/).

Consider HTML5 offline caches

In addition to ordinary caching, most modern browsers offer caches that are accessible even if a device isn't online. These caches are great because it's common for users even in developed areas to experience temporary loss of connectivity (say, going underground on the subway, or out of signal range on a mobile network). HTML5's application cache is one incredibly easy way to prepare a site for offline use. To use application cache, add a file to your website with a name like `example.appcache`, and reference it from your HTML file(s) like so:

```
<html manifest="example.appcache">
```

The contents of that `example.appcache` file tell the browser which assets it should cache for offline use and which assets it should always request over the network. For instance, to cache files for offline use, you might include the following in your `example.appcache` file:

```
CACHE MANIFEST
index.html
styles.css
logo.jpg
scripts.js
```

This instructs the browser to make `index.html`, `styles.css`, `logo.jpg`, and `scripts.js` available if you try to load them when offline. Of course, you can use application cache to support more complicated and nuanced scenarios as well. Application cache and other related browser features like local storage and the upcoming Service Worker API (http://bkaprt.com/rrd/3-19/) make it possible to specify how and which features of a site should work offline and which ones require a web connection (like making a credit card payment).

Offline access can be helpful to our users in the most critical moments, so enabling it is something we should always consider, especially for basic sites where the effort to do so can be low. For more on application cache, visit HTML5 Rocks (http://bkaprt.com/rrd/3-20/).

Automating all the things

While you could manage the above techniques manually, I don't recommend it. Recently, tools for automating these tasks have

FIG 3.12: CodeKit with a number of tasks configured (http://bkaprt.com/rrd/3-21/).

improved dramatically; if you're not using them, you're really missing out. Here are a couple that are worth your time.

CodeKit

CodeKit is a Mac desktop application that provides a number of common build-related tasks that you can run, like optimizing images, concatenating and minifying files, running preprocessors like Sass, and much more (**FIG 3.12**).

Grunt

For those who aren't afraid to dig into the command line a bit, Grunt is a JavaScript-driven task runner that you can configure to run as many build process tasks as you'd like, such as concatenating and minifying CSS and JavaScript files, copying and manipulating the file system, and even generating icons (**FIG 3.13**).

FIG 3.13: Find all of the officially supported tasks on the Grunt website and on GitHub (http://bkaprt.com/rrd/3-22/).

4 DELIVERING RESPONSIBLY

NOW THAT WE'VE prepared our files for production, let's examine how to responsibly deliver them: HTML, CSS, images, fonts, and JavaScript.

DELIVERING HTML

Earlier, we learned that the average website today weighs around 1.7 megabytes. Of that weight HTML contributes a relatively small share, about 55 kilobytes, but its size doesn't tell the entire story of its impact on perceived and total load time. As with most client-side technologies, every line of HTML carries the possibility of references to external assets that must be requested over a network (like images and video), each with its own size and timing implications.

Mobile-first content

In Luke Wroblewski's 2009 post "Mobile First" (which preceded his A Book Apart book of the same name), he points out that designing for devices that have tight screen-size constraints forces you to focus on the most important data and actions: "There simply isn't room in a 320 by 480 pixel screen for extraneous, unnecessary elements. You have to prioritize" (http://bkaprt.com/rrd/4-01/).

Ideally, we want to deliver only the content and functionality that our users desire, regardless of their devices. In practice, this can mean applying some content triage to our pages or screens. Scan your pages for content that isn't essential to each page's primary purpose, like teasers from external articles, social media tie-ins, comments, and ads. Such auxiliary content may not be necessary when pages are first delivered; delivering it up front can add to the time it takes for pages to become usable, especially on a slow connection.

It's helpful to identify what portions of the content are absolutely necessary and load the rest later on, after the essentials have been served. This practice is known as *deferred* or *lazy* loading.

Deferred content loading for better perceived performance

If a piece of supplementary content is already accessible in its own dedicated place elsewhere on the site, that piece may be a good candidate for deferred loading. In other words, as long as you can get to content through a click or two, consider its presence on other pages a user convenience—a nice bonus that isn't crucial (contrary to what the marketing department may tell you).

Configuring our pages to serve critical content first can lead to a faster initial page load. To load auxiliary content, we can then use JavaScript after the page is presented to the user.

Implementing conditional loading

Two of the best articles proposing the idea of lazy-loading HTML in responsive designs are "Conditional Loading for Responsive

Designs" (http://bkaprt.com/rrd/4-02/) and "Clean Conditional Loading" (http://bkaprt.com/rrd/4-03/), both by web standards genius Jeremy Keith. These articles offer JavaScript patterns for loading a fragment of HTML into an existing page based on the size of the browser's viewport.

Around the same time Keith wrote these articles, we released our own approach called Ajax-Include (http://bkaprt.com/rrd/4-04/). The Ajax-Include pattern can be used to lazy-load content in qualified environments, allowing you to deliver a streamlined version of the content—a link to a section of the site, for example—and replace that link with a fragment of HTML from that section after the page has loaded.

Hypothetically, we could choose to apply the Ajax-Include pattern to the feature wells on the *Boston Globe* homepage shown in **FIG 4.1**. Each well consists of a link to a major section (Sports, Metro, Columnists) and teaser content from that section's front page: links to stories, images, and videos, etc. The basic markup for the links that start each well would look something like this:

```
<a href="/sports">Sports</a>
```

If we want to dynamically include the content following each feature-well link, we can amend this markup to ready it for the Ajax-Include pattern. To do so, we need to incorporate one or two HTML5 data attributes, which are new customizable attributes we can use on any HTML element to store data. Although they do nothing on their own, data attributes provide a convenient means of defining configuration information for our scripts (and thereby simplify ongoing maintenance). Syntactically speaking, data attributes are open-ended attribute names that start with `data-` and end with anything we like (e.g., `data-foo`).

We designed the Ajax-Include script to look for specific HTML5 data attributes used for fetching and appending content: `data-append`, `data-replace`, `data-after`, and `data-before`. These attribute names instruct the script to append content in one of several potential locations once it has been fetched:

Sports →   BASEBALL   FOOTBALL   BASKETBALL   HOCKEY

John Farrell brings a different tone to Red Sox camp
The difference in style between the new manager and Bobby Valentine is hard to miss.

Sabres seize control in third, beat Bruins

Ortiz, Napoli part-time participants for Red Sox

Kevin Garnett clarifies comments on All-Star Game

Patrice Bergeron taking more shots for Bruins

NASCAR ramps up curb appeal of next generation car

Metro →   OBITUARIES   NORTH   SOUTH   WEST

Brookline students track asteroid, set up live feed
As a massive asteroid made its way toward Earth, three students closely tracked the 150-foot-wide object through one of the largest telescopes in the Boston area.

UMass tops list of state's high earners

Utilities' storm response seen as improved

Detox unit closing plan draws opposition

Patrick fights Rotenberg shock therapy decree

Senate hopeful critical of bin Laden spy leaks

Columnists   ›

LAWRENCE HARMON
Degrees of disappointment

DAN SHAUGHNESSY
Carl Crawford, Adrian Gonzalez still complaining about Boston

SCOT LEHIGH
GOP progress — now you see it, now you don't

KEVIN CULLEN
Whitey-washed disinformation

FIG 4.1: Section wells on the *Boston Globe* homepage.

- `data-append` appends the content at the end of the referencing element.
- `data-replace` replaces the referencing element with the injected content.
- `data-before` and `data-after` inject the content before or after the referencing element.

By adding one of these custom HTML5 `data-after` attributes to our sports link, we can reference a URL that contains the content of that feature well, and instruct our JavaScript to request that content and insert it into the page.

```
<a href="/sports" data-after="/sports/ »
  homepage-well/">Sports</a>
```

Then we need to include the JavaScript. If you visit Filament Group's article on Ajax-Include, you'll find a link to download the script's source file hosted on GitHub (http://bkaprt.com/rrd/4-05/). Ajax-Include is dependent on jQuery (or a framework with similar syntax) as well, so you must reference both jQuery and Ajax-Include for it to work.

```
<!-- references to jQuery and Ajax-Include -->
<script src="jquery.js"></script>
<script src="ajaxinclude.js"></script>
```

After referencing these necessary JavaScript files, we write a line of JavaScript (in jQuery syntax) to instruct Ajax-Include to perform its logic on the elements we need. For example, this line of jQuery tells the browser to find any elements on the page that have a `data-after` attribute, and call the `ajaxInclude` plugin on them.

```
$( "[data-after]" ).ajaxInclude();
```

To configure all of the Ajax-Include uses you might need on a site with one command, I typically add the other available selectors to the command, too:

```
$( "[data-after],[data-before],[data-replace], »
  [data-append]" ).ajaxInclude();
```

Going back to our section wells example, the command above results in a before-and-after effect on the page (**FIG 4.2**).

FIG 4.2: Initial content and content after running Ajax-Include.

The benefits of this approach are persuasive. While it does indeed introduce additional HTTP requests, the requests are made after the initial page is rendered and usable, so people interact with parts of the page a little sooner. The pattern can also be optimized to include several pieces of content in a single request if needed, or perhaps even fetch the content as structured data if your API allows such niceties. Perhaps most interestingly, the content can be included—or not—based on a variety of conditions, since it's already a click away for all users.

Loading for some breakpoints but not others

Ajax-Include isn't necessarily intended to serve different content to different devices. That said, you can also specify that it fetch content only when a particular media query applies. To do so, specify a `data-media` attribute with any media query value, and the content will only be fetched if the media condition ever becomes valid (either at load time or later). For example, here's an Ajax-Include that applies when the viewport is wider than 35em. Smaller viewports receive a link to the Sports page, where they'll find this content anyway.

```
<a href="/sports" data-after="/sports/homepage-well/" »
  data-media="(min-width: 35em)">Sports</a>
```

Responsive source order

Another HTML challenge that sometimes arises when building complex responsive sites is that it's often difficult to achieve a specific layout due to the order of the elements within the HTML file, aka the source order. CSS layout using traditional tools like `float` and `clear` has been constrained by HTML source order from the beginning; only recently have features such as CSS Flexbox emerged to give us more control. Still, with upcoming approaches working only in the latest browsers, it's good to have a plan B—ideally, a plan that does not involve using device detection to serve different markup to different devices, or repeating markup in different parts of a page in order to show or hide content.

When layout is bound, AppendAround

If we have the markup we need but it's not in the right part of our document to achieve a particular layout, we can use JavaScript to move it from one location in the HTML to another. One approach to this is AppendAround (http://bkaprt.com/rrd/4-06/), which we built and used for the *Boston Globe* site. Let's look at an example: the following wireframe shows an ad that needs to be in different locations in the layout at different breakpoints (**FIG 4.3**).

Due to source-order constraints, placing the content in these two locations with traditional CSS alone is sometimes not feasible: the small-screen layout needs the ad high in the linear source order so that users see it as soon as they scroll down the page, while the wider layout needs the ad positioned midway down in the far-right column, much later in the source order following a block of text that may vary in height.

With the AppendAround technique, we can automatically move the ad from one place to another in the DOM based on whichever CSS breakpoint happens to be in play. **FIG 4.4** demonstrates how that works with a basic piece of content.

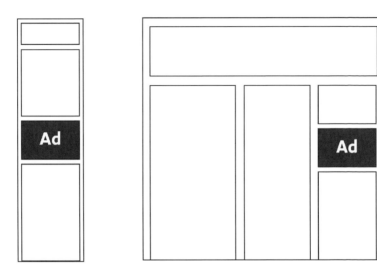

FIG 4.3: An example of AppendAround moving an ad unit in the DOM.

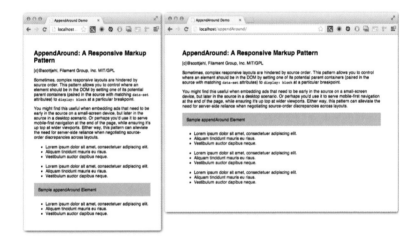

FIG 4.4: Example of a relatively unstyled roving content block using AppendAround (http://bkaprt.com/rrd/4-07/).

The HTML for AppendAround is pretty simple. Wherever you want a particular roving piece of content to appear in the document, create an empty container element with a data-set attribute whose value matches that of all other potential parents of that content piece, and apply that same attribute and value to the initial parent of the roving content as well. In the case below, the potential parent elements have the attribute data-set="rover-parent".

```
<!-- initial container for appendAround -->
<div class="rover-parent-a" data-set="rover-parent">
  <p class="rover">Sample appendAround Content</p>
</div>

<ul>
  <li>Lorem ipsum dolor sit amet.</li>
  <li>Vestibulum auctor dapibus neque.</li>
</ul>

<!-- potential container for appendAround -->
<div class="rover-parent-b" data-set="rover-parent">
</div>
```

Next we need to add the JavaScript that drives AppendAround, and then find our element on the page and call the appendAround() method on it.

```
<script src="jquery.js"></script>
<script src="appendAround.js"></script>
<script>
  /* Call appendAround */
  $( ".rover" ).appendAround();
</script>
```

Here's where things get interesting. In CSS, all we have to do is make one of the potential containers visible at a given breakpoint and the .rover element will be appended to that element. When the page loads, and whenever the viewport is resized, the script will check to see if an AppendAround element is hidden. If so, it will try to find a potential parent that is visible and append it there. Here's the CSS:

```css
.rover-parent-a {
  display: block;
}
.rover-parent-b {
  display: none;
}

@media ( min-width: 30em ){
  .rover-parent-a { display: none; }
  .rover-parent-b { display: block; }
}
```

That's it! With this technique, we're able to use CSS alone to direct where a piece of content is located in the DOM. One caveat, though: try to avoid using AppendAround for large, critical pieces of content, as it can sometimes cause the page to reflow around the newly appended element (which is something we want to minimize). Ideally, we should exhaust all options with CSS alone before resorting to workarounds like this. Still, it's nice to have them when we get stuck.

Now that we've discussed some approaches to cutting our HTML delivery costs, let's move on to talk about referenced assets. First up: CSS.

DELIVERING CSS

Among front-end assets, CSS requests have the highest correlation to the time it takes for a page to render (http://bkaprt.com/rrd/4-08/). Unfortunately, our CSS only stands to increase in size as the number of screen sizes and conditions we're addressing continues to grow.

While CSS offers plenty of ways to qualify the *application* of particular styles (media queries, conditional classes, @supports rules), it currently lacks mechanisms for qualifying its delivery to specific environments. Regardless, we can take steps to mitigate CSS overhead as best we can and prepare our CSS delivery so that it prioritizes perceived performance.

It's all in your head

As we learned in the last chapter, all styles required for the initial page layout should be referenced from a page's head; otherwise, we risk a FOUC during page load. From the head, we have a few typical ways to reference external styles.

Approach A: one big stylesheet containing inline media queries

Perhaps the most common approach to delivering responsive CSS is to concatenate all CSS into a single file, qualifying styles via media queries that apply under various conditions. The markup looks something like this:

```
<head>
...
<link href="all.css" rel="stylesheet">
...
</head>
```

The CSS within that stylesheet looks as you may expect:

```
/* first, some broad styles for all contexts */
body {
  background: #eee;
  font-family: sans-serif;
}
/* then, styles qualified to particular media */
@media (min-width: 35em){
   ...styles for viewport widths 35em (~560px) and up
}
@media (min-width: 55em){
   ...styles for viewport widths 55em (~880px) and up
}
```

First, the upsides. Combining all CSS into one file means it only requires one blocking HTTP request to fetch, and reducing the number of blocking requests is one of the best ways to speed up page delivery and reduce potential points of failure. Also, having all potentially applicable styles available allows the browser to apply styles immediately when conditions change, as with a device-orientation shift or browser resize.

On the downside, this approach can unnecessarily increase page-load time and chip away at data plans by requiring users to download styles that might never apply in their browser or device. Whether the overhead incurred by this approach is costly enough to consider alternatives depends on its overall weight and impact on perceived performance.

All things considered, the redundant syntax of CSS allows it to compress extremely well with Gzip, which helps mitigate the overhead of inapplicable styles.

Approach B: separate, media-specific files

A second method for loading responsive CSS is to separate styles for particular media into their own files and request those files independently. To specify the conditions in which each stylesheet should apply, we add `media` attributes to the `link` elements with media query values. Those `media` attributes work just like a media query inline in the CSS, so if you wanted to, you could remove the inline media queries inside the CSS files and the styles would still apply as expected.

```
<head>
...
<link href="shared.css" rel="stylesheet">
<link href="medium.css" media="(min-width: 35em)" »
  rel="stylesheet">
<link href="large.css" media="(min-width: 55em)" »
  rel="stylesheet">
</head>
```

The pros and cons of this approach depend on the browser. I'll start with the downside: if you've gotten your hopes up thinking that browsers will ignore stylesheets targeted with media queries that don't match their media conditions, allow me to disappoint. All common browsers today will request every single stylesheet referenced in an HTML document, regardless of whether their media attributes match or not (http://bkaprt.com/rrd/4-09/).

So much for using this approach to shave off some bytes. We've got another problem: we've added two blocking HTTP requests to load the same set of styles we were loading before. On top of that, separate files must be compressed separately for transfer, meaning the accumulated size of the CSS will likely be larger.

There is an upside, however. Several modern browsers like Safari (Mac and iOS), Opera, and Chrome will evaluate a `link` element's `media` attribute to check if its conditions apply to the current browsing environment, and then use that information to raise or lower the priority of that stylesheet's request. Low-priority requests won't block page rendering, which means that while all of the stylesheets will indeed be requested, these browsers will allow the page to render as soon as all applicable stylesheets have finished loading, letting the other stylesheets arrive at their convenience. **FIG 4.5** and **FIG 4.6** demonstrate the effects of traditional versus more modern approaches to loading inapplicable CSS media.

Whether this up-and-coming browser behavior is worth using depends on a few factors. If large portions of your CSS are targeted at particular environments or breakpoints, rather than being shared across many, this approach may allow your site to load faster in some browsers than a single stylesheet containing all files. However, given that many popular browsers don't yet handle the requests of inapplicable stylesheets as lower priorities, it may be best to stick to approach A. The only way to know is to test some real browsers and compare results.

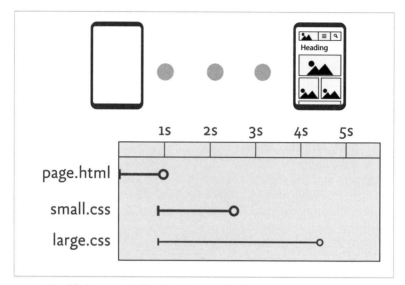

FIG 4.5: Simplified request timeline for a browser that does not treat inapplicable CSS as a low priority.

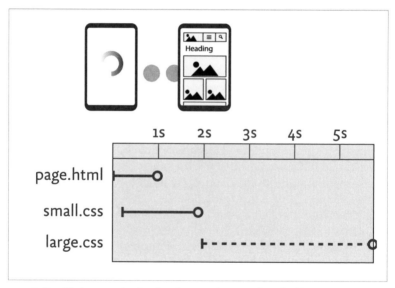

FIG 4.6: Simplified request timeline for a browser that treats inapplicable CSS as a low priority.

Approach C: everything inline

A third approach inlines the CSS into the HTML document itself:

```
<head>
  ...
  <style>
    /* first, some broad styles for all contexts */
    body {
      background: #eee;
      font-family: sans-serif;
    }
    /* then, styles qualified to particular media */
    ...
  </style>
</head>
```

The pros and cons of this are pretty straightforward. Just like approach A, including all the CSS in one place allows it to compress well for transfer. Additionally, approach C enables us to load all of our CSS without making a separate HTTP request to get it, which likely makes this approach load faster upon an initial visit. On the downside, inlining styles into the HTML removes a browser's ability to cache those styles as its own asset for future page loads, so that same set of styles needs to load anew with each page visited.

As a standalone strategy, I recommend only doing this when you're building a single-page website, or if the CSS for each page is different (which would be unusual), or if the entire CSS for your site is minimal (say, less than 8 kilobytes).

What's best?

It's complicated.

For responsive sites that share a majority of their CSS rules across browsers and devices, approach A is likely the most responsible way to deliver CSS. However, as we continue to add CSS for vastly different types of devices in the future and browsers continue to improve, we'll likely find that approach B is a better option. Unfortunately, both A and B require blocking external requests, which approach C successfully avoids—but only at the cost of reduced caching.

There has to be a better way! Perhaps a hybrid approach of C and B would be best of all...

A hybrid winner emerges

An increasingly popular tactic to consider with regard to perceived performance is the idea of optimizing for the very first network round-trip to the server, which carries about 14 kilobytes of data back to the browser. If you can manage to fit the HTML, CSS, and JavaScript necessary to render the above-the-fold (an imprecise metric for the top portion of the page) content in that first round-trip, you're nearly guaranteed to hit the one-second perceived page-load time we all aspire to. To reach that goal, Google's PageSpeed Insights tool (http://bkaprt.com/rrd/4-10/) recommends that we try to inline only the CSS critical for rendering content in the initial view, and load the rest in a non-blocking way. Of course, the fold varies from screen to screen, and it's difficult to know for sure which parts of our CSS will be critical and which parts won't. One plausible approach may be to organize our stylesheets in order—top to bottom, outside-in—according to where components sit in the page. We could start by inlining much of the layout for the top portion of the page, and make a judgement call about the point at which we should request the rest externally in a non-blocking manner.

Let's say we have a layout where the top of the page across all breakpoints consists of a masthead, navigation, and featured content, with other components like secondary content features and a footer below. In that case, we might set up the inline CSS in our page's head like this:

```
<head>
  ...
  <style>
    /* critical CSS styles for this template go
    here... */
  </style>
  ...
</head>
```

With this in place, we'll have no blocking CSS requests in the head of the page, and we may be able to get much of the top of the page into that first 14-kilobyte round-trip to the server.

Manually managing CSS files this way can be tricky, though, so I recommend using a tool to get the job done right. In his article "Detecting Critical Above-the-fold CSS," Paul Kinlan offers a bookmarklet you can run on any page to extract its critical styles (http://bkaprt.com/rrd/4-11/). Kinlan's logic is simple: critical CSS is the subset of CSS rules required to render the top portion of a page at a given viewport size. For responsive sites, I like to run this bookmarklet at a large viewport size, say 1200 by 900 pixels, so that I can capture the styles needed to render a responsive layout's many breakpoints.

Bookmarklets are nice, but for a large-scale codebase you'll want something more automated. To that end, my colleague Jeff Lembeck and I built a tool called Grunt-CriticalCSS (http://bkaprt.com/rrd/4-12/) that automatically extracts critical CSS for every template and writes it to a file that can be included inline. When properly configured, Grunt-CriticalCSS runs invisibly in the background every time you change a CSS file, keeping your critical CSS files up to date at all times.

No matter which tool you use to generate your critical CSS, once it's generated you'll want to include it directly in the page's head element. As for the site's full CSS, you'll want to load that in a non-blocking manner as quickly as possible.

To do this, you can use a JavaScript function called loadCSS (http://bkaprt.com/rrd/4-13/), which loads CSS files asynchronously so that they don't block page rendering. In keeping with our goal of eliminating blocking requests, `loadCSS` is small enough to include inline in the `head`. Also, I recommend placing the script that will contain `loadCSS` *after* your `style` element, as that order allows the JavaScript to insert the site's full CSS after the inline CSS, avoiding potential specificity conflicts. The overall approach looks something like this:

```
<style>
  /* critical CSS styles for this template go here... */
</style>
<script>
  // first, include the loadCSS function inline
  function loadCSS( href ){ ... }
  //then pass it a reference to a stylesheet to load
  loadCSS( "full.css" );
</script>
```

To be safe, I recommend following that last style element with a link to the site's full CSS that can still be requested when JavaScript is unavailable. Here's how that looks:

```
<noscript><link href="full.css" rel="stylesheet">
</noscript>
```

This is an admittedly intricate but overall worthwhile way to optimize how you load CSS. We'll revisit this approach at the end of the chapter when we combine it with others to fully enhance a page.

Regardless of the CSS delivery approach you take, aim to write CSS that is as concise as possible, taking advantage of the cascade to reduce repetition. Always minify (remove white space and comments with a tool like Grunt-CSS) the CSS in each file, and transfer all external CSS files with Gzip compression enabled.

DELIVERING IMAGES

When it comes to file size, images are the worst offenders. Out of that 1.7-megabyte average website, images take up 61%. The problem only continues to worsen as device sizes and resolutions become more diverse.

Thankfully, unlike CSS and JavaScript, all browsers request images asynchronously, or without blocking page rendering, by default. But while pending image requests don't block the page from rendering, they still cause serious performance issues. Many of those problems stem from the images' sheer weight, which causes them to load slowly and eat away at even the most generous data plan.

To begin our exploration of how we can load responsive imagery responsibly, let's talk about the difference between background images and foreground images.

Background images

Even when they're included in the background via CSS, images create HTTP requests. For example, the following rule causes a browser to request the image foo.jpg and render it in the background of all elements with a class of foo:

```
.foo {
  background: url(foo.jpg);
}
```

Straightforward enough. Things get slightly more interesting when we want to load different background images for different media conditions. Considering the grim options outlined in the CSS section, you may be surprised to find that it's actually quite simple to responsibly load background images with CSS and media queries. Research by Tim Kadlec demonstrated that most browsers in active use, when presented with two `background-image` rules applied to the same element, will fetch the last referenced image (http://bkaprt.com/rrd/4-14/). This works within media queries as well.

In the following example, browsers with a viewport of 30em or wider will request and render foo-large.jpg, while smaller browsers get foo.jpg.

```
.foo {
  background: url(foo.jpg);
}

@media (min-width: 30em){
  .foo {
    background: url(foo-large.jpg);
  }
}
```

Upgrading background images for HD screens

You can use this approach for any conditions that media queries support, which means you can easily use it to "upgrade" imagery for HD screens. The min-resolution media query lets us target devices with screens at or above a particular dpi (vendor-specific fallbacks such as -webkit-min-device-pixel-ratio help round out support here too). I've used 144dpi in this example because it's twice the standard screen definition of 72 dots per inch, and a good baseline for HD screens (which now often go even higher than 144 dots per inch).

```
.foo {
  background: url(foo.jpg);
}

@media (min-resolution: 144dpi){
  .foo {
    background: url(foo-large.jpg);
    background-size: 50px 50px;
  }
}
```

Note that `background-size` is included alongside the larger image to specify that the image should actually render at a size that may differ from its inherent dimensions. In this case, we'd like a larger image to fit within the same physical space as the standard definition image, which will pack more pixels into that space for a richer display. You may find with some imagery that the double-sized version of a particular image is already pretty light and responsible, and no negotiation is needed (this is sometimes true of artwork with few colors and gradients, for example). In that case, sending all devices the larger size with `background-size` specified may be a fine approach.

Inline data URIs

Another option is the data URI, which embeds an image's (or any file's) data directly into a string of gibberish that you can use in place of an external reference to that file, removing the need to make a request to the server for that asset. Here's an example of an arrow image encoded as a data URI:

```
data:image/png;base64,iVBORw0KGgoAAAANSUhEUgAAAoAAAAPCA
YAAADd/14OAAAABHNCSVQICAgIfAhkiAAAAlwSFlzAAALEwAACxMBAJ
qcGAAAAUFJREFUKJGV0C9MAnEUB/Dve3eMIptszuL43XE/1GgjOCduZp
3RrDSjVYPFzWR0jtnMMKPB2ZwUk8WheIdAcWM08QbvZzhRQAi+9rbP3p
+vlclk4tOJRHEmmWy22u0AE4pNGJ4TaLNrzI1W6fxkyHwrIiGDbJApaO
We5pCzRyEBgFZqGQYlMM8CgDFy3SPaDoKgPQQBwHVdx+rJFZiXAAAiT0
bsjWqjWgEA7kPf94N4Z2oFglJ0FC+SLWVPqfWhiYN3a8c5Aujgd63ZGw
ehlErGiFv93gBNHkXenDcfA+77vQAPVq+bHYLacdbIljKIF75VMdH5WK
3U642fvLRK5wVyxoAdRYTj6pt/GA2NnrG8lHtCjP0oFQktsnafa6+Xg9
tIp9wLMHYAQIy8M7D1Uqvd/YmC2BRE5BMwj0KUHYf+VV8xa3TEn/anuA
AAAABJRU5ErkJggg==
```

If that looks puzzling, it's okay—it's not meant for humans to read. But wait! The neat part is, if you paste that into a browser's URL bar, you'll see something similar to **FIG 4.7**.

The syntax for a data URI can be described more simply than it looks in code: it always starts with `data:`, which cues the browser that the URL itself includes file data, then 2-3 semicolon-separated pieces of information about the type of file it is (an

image/png file type with base64 encoding, for example), then a comma, and the raw data of that file:

```
data:[<MIME-type>][;charset=<encoding>][;base64],<data>
```

Of course, these get particularly useful when brought into our codebase in place of external images. For example, here's how you reference that data URI as a CSS background image (truncated for your sanity):

```
.menu {
  background: url( "data:image/ »
    png;base64,iVBORw0KGgo..." );
}
```

You can also embed the raw source of text files in a data URI. Here's an SVG file:

```
.header {
  background: url("data:image/svg+xml, »
    <svg viewBox='0 0 40 40' height='25' width='25' »
    xmlns='http://www.w3.org/2000/svg'> »
    <path fill='rgb(91, 183, 91)' d='M2.379,14.729L5 »
    .208,11.899L12.958,19.648L25.877,6.733L28.707, »
    9.561L12.958,25.308Z'/></svg>");
}
```

While we have many ways to retrieve a file's data URI, the simplest I've come across is a web-based drag-and-drop tool made by Boaz Sender of Boucoup, a web consultancy in Boston (**FIG 4.8**).

Compared to ordinary asset references, data URIs speed up performance because you don't need to request assets over the network. But including file data inline forfeits the possibility of downloading the file only when it's needed (for example, an external background image that applies to a specific media query). Further, overusing data URIs can cause trouble in some mobile devices (http://bkaprt.com/rrd/4-16/). For these reasons, reserve data URIs for universal assets that apply across devices and breakpoints.

One last note: data URIs aren't limited to background images; you can use them for foreground images too.

Responsive, responsible foreground images

Foreground images include any images referenced from the HTML that are intended to be part of the content: images that contribute meaning to a web page, like a photograph that pairs with a news article, as opposed to images used for visual decoration, like icons or background tiles.

As you likely recall from the tenets of responsive design, adding the following CSS rule will ensure that all img elements in a layout fill 100% of the width of their container element without scaling beyond the image's own dimensions:

```
img { max-width: 100%; }
```

Since images can't scale far beyond their dimensions without looking awful, web authors often include images at their largest

FIG 4.9: The same image in compressive quality (left), and as it appears after the browser scales its dimensions (right).

intended display and let the browser scale them down in smaller viewports. Unfortunately, this practice of serving large images to everyone isn't very responsible—people end up loading far more data than their device needs.

Problems with responsibly serving foreground images across disparate devices largely derive from HTML's inability (until recently) to serve different versions of an image depending on the size a device needs. Fortunately, we now have the tools to handle this well.

Compressive images

If you don't need anything except a single, scalable image, you might consider an interesting technique developed by Daan Jobsis that I've dubbed *compressive images* (http://bkaprt.com/rrd/4-17/) (**FIG 4.9**). This approach saves JPEG images at twice their intended viewing dimensions at terrible quality settings, and then lets the browser scale the images down to clear up any artifacts. Amazingly, this cuts the size of a file in half while

FIG 4.10: The W3C Responsive Images Community Group website (http://bkaprt.com/rrd/4-18/).

improving its sharpness on HD screens. You sort of need to see it to believe it, so be sure to follow the link.

Compressive images have drawbacks too: scaling down large images uses a fair amount of processing power and memory, so the approach may not, uh, scale well when used heavily across a page. It's also fairly limited in that the file size of the image will need to grow to accommodate higher screen resolutions, at the expense of lower-resolution screens that won't need the extra data. Compressive images best suit simple cases. Now, let's look at an option for a fuller-featured responsive image solution.

Responsive images with HTML

In 2012, a W3C Responsive Images Community Group (RICG), chaired by Mat Marquis, came together to define the use cases addressed by an ideal responsive image solution and to recommend new HTML features for implementing these images in browsers (**FIG 4.10**).

The group proposed the `picture` element and its related attributes such as `srcset`, `sizes`, `media`, and `type`, which, happily, have become full-fledged W3C standards and are supported by modern browsers as I write this book. These new features present huge benefits, so let's go over how we can use them today.

The picture element

Per the specification, "the `picture` element is an image container whose source content is determined by one or more CSS media queries" (http://bkaprt.com/rrd/4-19/). `picture` is a new HTML element, or series of elements, complete with its own attributes. The `picture` element's use of media queries makes it easy to serve variations of images that pair with visual breakpoints in a CSS layout. This is useful when you have foreground images that need to scale in unison with other elements in a layout.

A `picture` element contains a series of `source` elements followed by an `img` element. If that sounds familiar, that's because `picture` follows similar syntax to the existing HTML `video` and `audio` elements, which feature a `container` element and several `source` elements that reference possible sources for the parent element to use. In the case of `picture`, however, the `source` elements act as controllers for the URL that will be displayed by their sibling `img` element. Here's an example of a `picture` element with a few potential source images:

```
<picture>
  <source media="(min-width: 45em)" srcset="large.jpg">
  <source media="(min-width: 18em)" srcset="med.jpg">
  <img srcset="small.jpg" alt="...">
</picture>
```

The `source` elements are listed in order of largest first, with `media` attributes specifying the maximum viewport size at which they should be applied. While this order of `source` element parsing may seem counterintuitive to those accustomed to writing small-screen-first media queries in CSS, it's designed to match the order in the `video` and `audio` HTML elements' source selection. A browser will iterate over the `source` elements in order of appearance and stop when it encounters a `source` with a matching `media` attribute, then set the `img` element's source to a URL specified in the `source` element's `srcset` attribute. If no `source` elements end up matching, the `img` element's own attributes (such as `srcset`) will be used to determine its source.

What's a srcset anyway?

You may be thinking: "`srcset` sounds and looks an awful lot like `src` to me; what's the difference?" As the name implies, `srcset` is a new attribute designed to contain one or more potential source URLs for an image—but it does more than that. `srcset` has a huge advantage: it asks the browser to decide the most appropriate asset based on any criteria the browser deems relevant, such as viewport size, screen resolution, and even network speed or other environmental conditions like the amount of data remaining on a user's mobile subscription. In other words, while we can declare several potential images with `srcset`, the browser is allowed to treat these as suggestions. This characteristic unique to srcset is extremely convenient, because when you factor in all of the various viewport sizes and screen resolutions your images should support, it would be quite verbose to describe them with something more prescriptive, like media queries.

`srcset` attributes can be used either on `source` elements within a `picture` element, or on `img` elements themselves—even `img` elements that don't have a `picture` element wrapper. Unless you're trying to pair the sources of an image with media query breakpoints in a layout, you probably won't need a `picture` element at all. `srcset`'s values are comma-delimited; you can pair each value with a description of the image's dimensions (using `w` and `h` units representing pixel measurements of the image asset itself) to help the browser determine which image is most appropriate to display based on viewport size and screen resolution. For example, here's a `srcset` attribute with two potential image sources:

```
<img srcset="imgs/small.png 400w, »
  imgs/medium.png 800w" alt="...">
```

This img offers two source URLs, small.png (400px wide),
and medium.png (800px wide). Of course, srcset can be used
with a single image URL and no additional information, as I
showed on the source and img elements in my initial picture
element example. But using srcset to list multiple potential
sources for each source element within picture has a great
benefit: we can offer images that pair well with design breakpoints while letting the browser determine the resolution of an
image that best fits the device's screen quality. It's art direction
with HD support. Take this markup, for example, in which the
first URL listed for each source would display on a standard-
definition screen, while the second URL (highlighted in bold)
would apply to high-resolution screens:

```
<picture>
  <source media="(min-width: 45em)" srcset="large.jpg
    45em, large-2x.jpg 90em"> »
  <source media="(min-width: 18em)" srcset="med.jpg »
    18em, med-2x.jpg 36em"> »
  <img srcset="small.jpg 8em, small-2x.jpg 16em" »
    alt="...">
</picture>
```

Perhaps this is a good time to mention fallbacks. srcset is not
yet natively supported in many browsers. One solution would
be to allow the img to fall back to the text provided in the alt
attribute, but then most browsers today would not get an image.
If we want the image to work more broadly than that, we need
to either use some JavaScript to polyfill the srcset attribute or
add an old src attribute to our img. Despite its ease and great
support, however, adding the src attribute comes at a cost: most
browsers will fetch the image listed in that src even if they don't
end up using it, racking up wasteful overhead no one wants.
For now, that leaves us with the polyfill option, which I'll cover
in a moment.

Introducing the sizes attribute

If your reaction to these examples is, "These look great, but I wish they were more complicated," you're in luck! To further assist the browser in its decision-making process with picture and img sources, the new sizes attribute lets us suggest the size at which an image will be rendered in the layout at a given media query breakpoint. Like srcset, the sizes attribute syntax is also comma-delimited, this time with each value offering an optional media query and a width at which the image should be rendered by CSS when that media query is active. Here's that img example from earlier with sizes added:

```
<img
srcset="imgs/small.png 400w, imgs/medium.png 800w"
sizes="(max-width: 30em) 100%, 50%"
"alt="...">
```

Have I lost you? If so, don't worry—sizes took me a little while to grasp too. In plain English, the above sizes example declares the following:

- (max-width: 30em) 100%. When the viewport is 30em or narrower, the image's width will be 100% of the viewport's width.
- 50%. Otherwise, if the viewport is wider than 30em, the image's width will be 50% of the viewport's width.

Now, it's important to note that these widths won't actually *apply* to the image; they're merely cues to allow the browser to render the image as close to its intended dimensions as possible, which helps prevent reflows as the page layout is drawn.

Using picture with different types of images

I should cover one more attribute with picture, and that's type. On each source element within picture, you can use an optional type attribute to specify a file format. If the browser supports that file format, then the source will be used. The type value should be specified in the syntaxes that HTTP defines for a particular file; thus an SVG file's type would be specified as "image/svg+xml", while a WebP (a new, highly optimized image format that's slowly gaining browser support) image format's type would be "image/webp". Here's a picture example with a source offered in both WebP and JPEG formats:

```
<picture>
  <source media="(min-width: 18em)" srcset="med.webp" »
    type="image/webp">
  <source media="(min-width: 18em)" srcset="med.jpg">
  <img srcset="small.jpg" alt="...">
</picture>
```

In browsers that support WebP, this markup means big savings in transfer size due to the format's incredible compression.

Using HTML responsive images today

At time of writing, a handful of browsers—Chrome, Opera, and Firefox, with others hot on their heels—plan to support picture imminently. That's great, but it's a paltry subset of the browsers we need to care about in serving images to our users. To use picture's features today, we may need a adopt a transitional approach.

Picturefill is a lightweight JavaScript polyfill maintained by Filament Group and endorsed by the RICG to make the new picture element (and img attributes) work in browsers that don't yet support them (**FIG 4.11**). **FIGURE 4.12** shows the effect in use on the Microsoft website.

To include Picturefill on your site, you can use the following snippet, which includes a quick HTML5 shiv for the picture element before loading picturefill.js in a non-blocking manner:

```
<script>
  // Picture element HTML5 shiv
  document.createElement( "picture" );
</script>
<script src="picturefill.js" async></script>
```

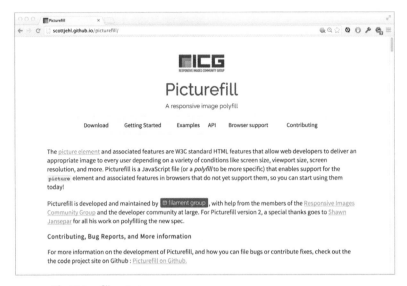

FIG 4.11: The Picturefill project.

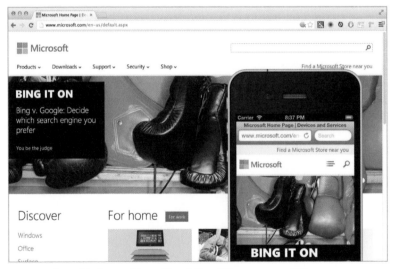

FIG 4.12: Microsoft's site uses Picturefill to deliver different crops to different viewport sizes.

FIG 4.13: Vector-based image editing.

You can find documentation, examples, and support information on the Picturefill project site (http://bkaprt.com/rrd/4-20/). The site also contains information about how the two versions of Picturefill deliver fallback imagery when JavaScript is unable to run, so be sure to compare the pros and cons of each version with your audience in mind.

ABANDONING THE PIXEL

The previous examples explore various ways to responsibly swap and negotiate bitmap imagery, as bitmaps are limited in their ability to scale across resolutions and dimensions. Of course, bitmaps aren't the only type of imagery available, and in many cases, they aren't the best tool for the task at hand. Because of the differences in viewport sizes and screen resolutions, it's ideal to have images that can scale without any decrease in quality. Luckily, most browsers today support a variety of scalable graphic formats. Let's look at a couple of ways to implement vector-based art on the web (**FIG 4.13**).

Icon fonts

One approach dates back to the early days of desktop computing: dingbat fonts, now often known as *icon fonts* (**FIG 4.14**). As a solution for presenting scalable images (especially smaller page elements), icon fonts have surged in popularity. And for good reason: they're widely available in free and paid packages online, and embedding them in a codebase is as simple as referencing any custom font. From a performance perspective, icon fonts

FIG 4.14: Screenshot of Chris Coyier's Icon Fonts preview page (http://bkaprt.com/rrd/4-21/).

are a great choice because the icons are delivered in a single font file via a single HTTP request, or no requests at all if the fonts are compacted into a data URI.

The trick with icon fonts is that we have to use them carefully, since they tend to gracelessly fail in browsers that don't support them. Let's look at an example of how to safely use them in a page. Here's the HTML:

```
<span><span class="icon-star" aria-hidden="true"> »
  </span>Favorite</span>
```

Now here's the CSS, in which we're using the @font-face feature to load a font file and assign it the font-family name "Icons". Later, we'll reference that font-family again when styling an element in the HTML:

```
@font-face {
  font-family: "Icons";
  src: url( "icons.woff" );
  font-weight: normal;
  font-style: normal;
}
.icon-star:before {
  font-family: "Icons";
  content: "★ ";
}
```

The clean, scalable result is shown in **FIGURE 4.15**.

Two things to note here. First, we've used a separate HTML element for the icon itself. This is deliberate: we want to be able to add an `aria-hidden` attribute to prevent the icon from being read aloud to users with assistive technology. (Yes, Unicode characters are read aloud, and the star above would read as "Black Star" on a screen reader such as VoiceOver.)

Second, we've used the `:before` pseudo-element to place the icon content in the page because it allows us to set its text content from CSS (via the `content` property), which isn't possible on ordinary elements. This is nice because it lets us keep visual style information, like the ★ character, out of our HTML and in our CSS where it belongs.

Bulletproofing the approach

As is the case with most technologies, icon fonts have some drawbacks. Browser support for CSS `@font-face` is pretty good, but it fails in unexpected ways in unsupported environments. For instance:

- Browsers like Android 2.3's native browser end up showing black squares where icons should be, which can cause usability problems when text isn't also available.
- Most icon fonts render blank in the popular proxy browser Opera Mini.

For these reasons, we need to include a feature test to bulletproof our approach. Zach Leatherman wrote a great article on the various things you should consider when using icon fonts; alongside the article he released a script to help us target icon fonts safely (http://bkaprt.com/rrd/4-22/). It's called A Font Garde (http://bkaprt.com/rrd/4-23/)—get it? Zach does a great job of explaining how to use the feature test, and I suggest you read the whole thing. But to summarize, the test adds a class of `supports-fontface` to the `html` element, which allows you to qualify your selectors like so:

```
.supports-fontface .icon-star:before {
    font-family: "Icons";
    content: "★ ";
}
```

And that's that!

In addition to being infinitely scalable and rendering sharply at any resolution, icon fonts can also be styled with CSS using the same styles that work for text. This means that icon fonts can be colored simply by assigning a CSS `color` property, or given a drop shadow treatment by using `text-shadow`.

From a design perspective, the major limitation of icon fonts is their current lack of support for multiple colors. It's a cinch to style the color of an entire icon with CSS, but there's no way to style portions of a font-generated icon differently. Workarounds do exist, such as stacking many characters to create layered multicolor icons (http://bkaprt.com/rrd/4-24/) or using `text-shadow`s to replicate a two-color icon, but the limitation is difficult to avoid.

Fortunately, if you'd like to use multiple colors or vector graphic elements other than icons, we have another scalable technology at our disposal.

FIG 4.16: The SVG example code renders as a star graphic.

Working with SVG

Scalable Vector Graphics, or SVG, is a complex and versatile markup language similar to HTML, but designed for drawing shapes. SVG has actually had great browser support for years, but a lack of native SVG support in Internet Explorer 8 and older held it back from mainstream use. With improved support, however, SVG has seen a huge surge in interest. Given its depth of features, it's easy to understand why. SVG not only scales beautifully across screen densities, but its elements are styleable via CSS, and as a text format it compresses very well with Gzip, so we can responsibly send it over the wire.

Let's look at a basic SVG example. The following code snippet produces a black star:

```
<svg>
  <polygon fill="black" points="6.504,0 8.509,4.068 »
    13,4.722 9.755,7.887 10.512,12.357 6.504,10.246 »
    2.484,12.357 3.251,7.887 0,4.722 4.492,4.068 ">
</svg>
```

Rendered in a browser, it appears as a clean graphic (**FIG 4.16**).

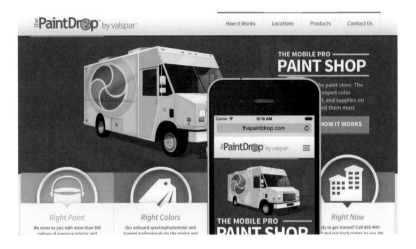

FIG 4.17: The Paint Drop's graphics are delivered as SVG, allowing them to render sharply with a small transfer size on any SD and HD screens.

Similar to HTML, the SVG document begins with an outermost wrapper element (`svg` in this case), which contains any number of standard child elements (`line`, `circle`, `path`, `polygon`, etc.), each with attributes describing the element's visual properties. In our example, the `polygon` element is used to create the star. Its `fill` attribute describes its fill color of `black`, and the `points` attribute contains a series of comma-delimited coordinates representing the points that connect the lines of the polygon.

Beyond such examples, SVG can get dramatically complex, with features for gradients, linking, blending modes and filters, and even animation. Graphics editors like Adobe Illustrator can open, manipulate, and save SVG, allowing designers to work directly with the files that are delivered over the web (**FIG 4.17**).

If you're a designer, you may be interested in optimal ways to build SVG graphics effectively using common design tools like Adobe Illustrator or Sketch. If so, I highly recommend checking out Todd Parker's slide deck "Leaving Pixels Behind," from a talk he gave at Artifact Conference in 2014 (**FIG 4.18**).

There are several ways to serve SVG files on the web, both as foreground and background images. Here are a few.

SVG as an img

Serving SVG via the `img` element is a convenient approach for inserting vector-based foreground images such as logos. You can reference an SVG file directly from an `img`'s `src` attribute (`<img src="star.svg" alt="...">`). But make sure you account for browsers that don't support SVG. To do this, include a `picture` element with its `type` attribute feature, along with Picturefill—so browsers will receive either the SVG or a fallback PNG:

```
<picture>
  <source type="image/svg+xml" srcset="star.svg">
  <img srcset="star.png" alt="...">
</picture>
```

SVG in your HTML

Embedding SVG markup directly in an HTML document offers loads of interesting opportunities, such as reusing artwork throughout a page, styling portions of the SVG in any number of ways with CSS, and even animating the paths and shapes within the SVG. To embed SVG in a document, just paste that SVG markup anywhere in the body of your page and it'll render in any supporting browser:

```
<body>
...
  <svg>
    <polygon fill="black" points="6.504,0 8.509,4.068 »
      13,4.722 9.755,7.887 10.512,12.357 6.504,10.246 »
      2.484,12.357 3.251,7.887 0,4.722 4.492,4.068">
  </svg>
...
```

Once in the page, you can style the SVG's elements with CSS, like so:

```
svg polygon {
  fill: red;
}
```

And that's just the start! Two articles in particular demonstrate the power of embedded SVG markup. The first is Jake Archibald's "Animated Line Drawing in SVG," which describes how you can animate the paths in an SVG line drawing with a little JavaScript and some CSS transitions (http://bkaprt.com/rrd/4-26/) (**FIG 4.19**).

The second article is "Icon System with SVG Sprites," in which Chris Coyier demonstrates the def and use features of SVG that allow variable-like reuse of artwork throughout a page (http://bkaprt.com/rrd/4-27/) (**FIG 4.20**).

Embedding SVG directly in HTML does have a couple drawbacks. One is a lack of ability to cache the SVG graphic as a standalone asset; the other is the overhead of sending SVG markup to browsers that might not be able to render it. If it's a small graphic, however, you might consider using a feature test like the one provided by Modernizr to hide the SVG elements and show a fallback image instead.

SVG as an object

Serving SVG via the object element retains the advantages of embedding SVG in HTML while improving the ability to cache the SVG file for use across a site:

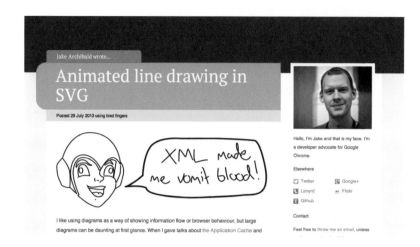

FIG 4.19: Jake Archibald's article "Animated Line Drawing in SVG."

```
<object data="star.svg" type="image/svg+xml">
...Fallback content goes here.
</object>
```

SVG as a background image

Last, you can also reference SVG files from CSS as background images:

```
.star {
  background: url(star.svg);
}
```

SVG URLs can alternatively be expressed as pure data as well, which we explored in the data URIs section earlier. Here's the star SVG embedded as a background image:

```
.star {
  background: url( "data:image/svg+xml, »
    <svg><polygon fill=\"black\" points=\"6.504,0 »
```

FIG 4.20: Chris Coyier's article "Icon System with SVG Sprites."

```
    8.509,4.068 13,4.722 9.755,7.887 10.512,12.357 »
    6.504,10.246 2.484,12.357 3.251,7.887 0,4.722 »
    4.492,4.068 \"/></svg>" );
}
```

Another HTTP request saved! But be careful not to place too many of these data URIs in a layout-blocking CSS file: their file size will contribute to a slower page-load time. (The key there is avoiding the layout-blocking part, which we'll cover next.)

Given that we can embed SVG background images this way, it's feasible to create an entire stylesheet containing nothing but SVG backgrounds, similar in benefits to the age-old CSS sprites technique that combined many bitmaps into one, but with vector graphics. This concept inspired us to create Grunticon (http://bkaprt.com/rrd/4-28/), a workflow tool for generating SVG sprite sheets from a folder of SVG source files.

Automating SVGs with Grunticon

Running on top of the Grunt task-runner utility, Grunticon makes it easy to manage and deliver sharp and scalable icons

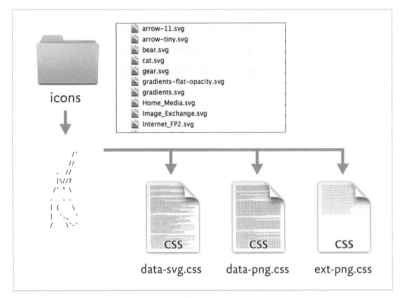

FIG 4.21: A diagram of the Grunticon workflow.

and background images across devices. It takes a folder of SVG files and outputs them to CSS files that define class names for each icon image. The CSS is exported in three files that contain the icon imagery in one of three formats: SVG data URIs, PNG data URIs, and externally referenced PNG images, which are also automatically created and placed in a folder. In addition, Grunticon generates a small bit of JavaScript and CSS that you can drop into your site to asynchronously load the appropriate icon CSS depending on a browser's capabilities, as well as a preview HTML file with that loader script in place (**FIG 4.21**).

Grunticon is one of many ways you can easily work with SVG in your web production workflow, and it's continually being improved.

Getting Grumpy

While Grunticon's command-line interface offers great opportunities for automation in a team's workflow, its setup and

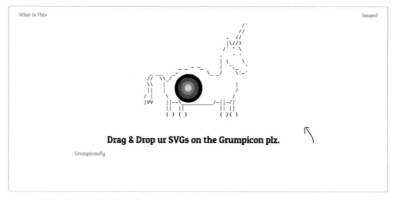

FIG 4.22: The Grumpicon interface.

configuration can be a challenge for those unfamiliar with the terminal. With that in mind, we created a web app companion to Grunticon called Grumpicon (http://bkaprt.com/rrd/4-29/)—which, allow me to point out, features an ASCII unicorn cantering across the screen, and also happens to convert SVG files into browser-ready Grunticon assets just like the command-line tool (**FIG 4.22**). To use it, visit the site, drag and drop your SVG files onto the page, and download your production-ready code.

DELIVERING FONTS

Support for web fonts has exploded in the past few years, and yet responsible font delivery still faces some thorny challenges. For starters, default font-loading behavior varies across browsers. If we reference font styles directly via a `link` element, not only do we introduce a potential point of failure as with any other blocking CSS request, but we also have to contend with issues like the potentially jarring *flash of unstyled text* (FOUT).

Yet another FOU

Since we've already covered asynchronous loading and the dreaded flash of unstyled content (FOUC), we'd be remiss to forget their most recent counterpart. FOUT happens whenever

FIG 4.23: Screenshot of Firefox and Opera browsers' font-loading behavior as seen on *STET* (http://bkaprt.com/rrd/4-30/). The FOUT is scarcely noticeable; fallback fonts appear (left) until custom fonts load (right).

an HTML page is displayed before its custom web fonts have finished loading. Because it happens natively in some browsers but not others, FOUT is a tricky beast—spurring debate on whether it's a feature or a bug (I'm in the feature camp).

The behavior works like this: in several browsers, including Firefox and Opera, the browser won't wait (at least not very long) for web fonts to load before rendering the page without them, deploying fallback fonts for text that otherwise would be styled with custom fonts. If and when the preferred fonts arrive, they will be applied as instructed by the CSS, instantly appearing throughout the page in place of the fallback fonts. This substitution often occurs seconds after the page is first displayed. The downsides are a potentially disorienting glitch for users, as well as repaints and reflows for the browser, which undermine performance. That said, the ability to declare appropriate fallback fonts in CSS allows us to lessen the pain FOUT can cause. A very subtle change in layout before and after custom fonts have loaded characterizes the FOUT at *STET* (FIG 4.23).

Making the FOUT this subtle involves careful typographic decisions that certainly aren't common across the web, however. In an effort to avoid FOUT entirely, browsers like Chrome, Safari, and Internet Explorer will display the page with invisible text until custom fonts have finished loading (FIG 4.24). I like to refer to this as a *Flash of Invisible Type* (FOIT). Advocates of FOIT describe it as a lesser evil, arguing that it is less jarring for users

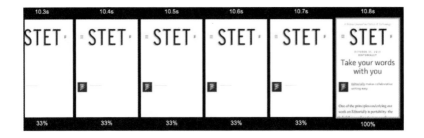

FIG 4.24: Screenshot of WebKit-derived browsers' font-loading behavior: no text at all until the font finishes loading.

to see no type at all than to see temporarily unstyled type. There are some downsides to FOIT as well, though, and they might even outweigh the disadvantages of the problem they attempt to fix. Most problematic is the time a FOIT browser will wait for a font to load before displaying fallback text, which can be upward of thirty seconds. Thirty seconds is a geological era in internet time, so as long as this behavior is common in browsers, it may be best to take steps to avoid it.

For what it's worth, at the time of writing it appears that Google is considering changing its behavior in favor of a much shorter timeout, like Firefox has. Until all the WebKit derivatives update, however (Android 2, anyone?), we'll be seeing FOIT on the web.

Avoiding FOIT, embracing FOUT

While FOIT behavior does come standard in many browsers, it typically occurs when custom fonts are loaded from CSS referenced in the head of a page's HTML. This is because the browser will only hide the text in a page if it expects an as-yet-to-be-loaded font in the near future. In light of this, we can avoid FOIT entirely and introduce a FOUT instead by loading font-referencing CSS files asynchronously via JavaScript. Loading fonts this way may present an acceptable compromise: the first time users visit a page, they may see a brief FOUT in all browsers, but any pages loaded after that will likely display no such issues: the browser's caching will usually ensure that the fonts are available immediately without making an external request. To pull this off, I recommend converting each of your custom fonts into data URIs and packing them into a single CSS file along with their `font-face` definitions. (If you're serving your fonts in several formats, you'll want to package fonts of each format in their own files and load files depending on the browser's support.) The advantage of delivering fonts as data inside a single CSS file is that doing so eliminates the time between when a `font-face` is defined and when it's loaded, thus minimizing the likelihood of FOIT. Once you have your fonts combined in a file, you can use the same `loadCSS` function I referenced in the CSS loading section earlier:

```
<head>
  ...
  // Load fonts.css in a non-blocking manner!
  loadCSS( "fonts.css" );
  ...
</head>
```

Of course, you might want to use some logic to decide which of many files to include based on the type of fonts a browser supports—WOFF, TrueType, SVG, etc. For a robust font-loading plan, you might also check out the new font-loading APIs landing in browsers today (http://bkaprt.com/rrd/4-31/).

Beyond delivering a usable page as early as possible, there are plenty of other things to consider when it comes to web font usage, but they are of course beyond the scope of this book. For a deeper dive into web type, I humbly refer you to Jason Santa Maria's *On Web Typography*.

DELIVERING JAVASCRIPT

Looking back at our 1.7-megabyte website, JavaScript is the second largest slice of pie, sliding in after images at 282 kilobytes. The entire operating system that drove the Apollo 11 mission to the moon weighed 64 kilobytes. What are we doing with this logic?! Sweet fly-out menus is what.

Beyond its size, JavaScript packs a serious anti-performance punch. As discussed earlier, JavaScript blocks page rendering—by default at least—while it's requested and parsed, which means the more scripts we have, the longer our users need to wait for a usable site. This blocking behavior produces problems similar to those we experience when loading CSS. JavaScript, though, has a number of capabilities that enable it to be responsibly loaded more easily.

"'We don't have any non-JavaScript users.' No, all your users are non-JS while they're downloading your JS."
—JAKE ARCHIBALD, http://bkaprt.com/rrd/4-32/

We can take several steps to achieve great perceived and actual performance with our JavaScript, in how we both write and deliver it. First, let's explore the problems we face with JavaScript size and delivery.

Our conveniences are showing

JavaScript has a reputation as a hefty asset, but it doesn't end up that way on its own. The language is dynamic and flexible, and it does a lot with a bit of code. The problem is that JavaScript has historically ping-ponged between different, non-standard implementations, causing us to write the same code in multiple ways and compounding complexity and file size to depressing effect. The suggestions below will help you fight bloat as you make your page as fast as it can be.

Consider JS a tertiary enhancement

Whenever possible, it's best to piggyback on native HTML and CSS to do our heavy lifting and consider JavaScript a last resort. That's because JavaScript tends to be our least reliable layer of enhancement: one syntax error makes it fail completely, while HTML and CSS handle hiccups more gracefully. Always try to determine whether behavior or presentation can be achieved with HTML and CSS alone.

Question whether a library is necessary at all

DOM libraries like jQuery offer ways to query, traverse, and manipulate HTML elements via CSS selectors (among many other things). Due to their *write-once-run-everywhere* methods, these libraries became popular in an era when it was difficult to do anything across browsers. In the past few years, however, JavaScript browser support has improved so dramatically that large portions of libraries are sometimes no longer needed. Perhaps the greatest boost that JavaScript has received in modern browsers is support for the `querySelectorAll` method, which allows us to query the DOM for elements using CSS selectors, just as we do with jQuery!

```
var h3Subs = document.querySelectorAll( "h3.sub-hed" );
```

Also arriving in browsers are new APIs for easily adding and removing class names, iterating over loops, extending objects, and more. With broader support for these features, our need to include large normalization libraries is slowly disappearing, so always consider whether the cost of sending enhancements to legacy browsers is necessary. If you decide to go ahead without a library, take steps to prevent your script from loading or executing in older browsers that won't understand it. (We'll get to that shortly.)

Consider a simple DOM framework

If you're building a complex site, it often pays to use some sort of JavaScript framework; such frameworks offer common convenience functions to keep your code maintainable. That said, there are many small DOM frameworks that offer the same conveniences without the heft. One that has worked well for our projects (we've used it on sites for LEGO, among others) is called Shoestring (http://bkaprt.com/rrd/4-33/), which was built at Filament Group and is now largely maintained by my coworker John Bender, who may or may not be a robot (*the guy is quite sharp*). Essentially, Shoestring is a DOM framework on a budget—it's built for speed (**FIG 4.25**).

FIG 4.25: The Shoestring project on GitHub.

Shoestring mimics jQuery's code syntax, but that's where the similarities end. Designed to be extremely minimal, Shoestring contains only a fraction of the methods in jQuery, nearly all of them written so they can be excluded from a build if you don't need them. Because it weighs only a few kilobytes, it's great for performance, but there are occasions when Shoestring's feature set falls short of your needs. Fortunately, any JavaScript you write based on Shoestring will work in jQuery, so you can always swap in jQuery in a pinch (say, at 5 p.m. on a Friday).

Making a custom jQuery build

Definitely still need jQuery? Fair enough. You can at least try to make jQuery smaller. jQuery now allows you to create custom builds that exclude many modules from its codebase. Depending on how much jQuery you need, the core can be as small as 12 kilobytes, after minification and Gzip. For information on how to make a custom build, check out this guide (http://bkaprt.com/ rrd/4-34/).

Ready to go!

After optimizing our JavaScript dependencies, we can focus on loading our JavaScript responsibly. Let's look at how best to do so.

Options for loading JavaScript

Remember, any `script` element referencing an external file will block subsequent content from rendering until that file has finished loading and executing. This undesirable blocking behavior can be mitigated or prevented depending on how we choose to load scripts.

Taking it from the top

Likely the simplest and most common approach to loading JavaScript is via a `script` element within the head of a document.

```
<head>
   ...
   <script src= "myscript.js" ></script>
   ...
</head>
```

The behavior is straightforward: any JavaScript-supporting browser will fetch `myscript.js` and run it upon arrival. Requests to JavaScript files referenced this way are often made concurrently, but the order in which the scripts are executed is preserved based on the order that they appear in the DOM. This makes for a convenient approach to loading several scripts that may or may not depend on one another:

```
<head>
   ...
   <script src="myjslibrary.js"></script>
   <script src="myscript.js"></script>
   ...
</head>
```

Another benefit to this approach is that assets referenced in the page source at the start are exposed to the browser's parser early in the page-load process, and are therefore fetched as soon as possible.

Of course, the drawbacks are plentiful. This approach offers no means of qualifying the conditions on which a script should be requested and executed (any JavaScript-supporting browsers will do both, in this case), and scripts referenced this way delay page rendering until they have finished loading and executing. In rare cases, blocking rendering until a particular script has finished running is desirable or even necessary. For example, when executing shims, polyfills, feature tests, or other scripts that dramatically modify the ways in which the page is rendered, referencing them from the head makes pages load more smoothly.

In these cases, we do want a portion of our JavaScript to appear in the head of a page, but we still don't want to delay page load while that JavaScript is requested over the network. So let's look at another option for including JavaScript in the head that avoids making any requests at all.

Inlining in the head

One solution to the network latency problem is to *inline* JavaScript in the head of the page. Inlining JavaScript this way allows it to execute as soon as the HTML is parsed, which is a nice alternative to waiting for it to be fetched externally. Here's an inlined script:

```
<head>
  ...
  <script>
  /* JavaScript source code goes here... */
  </script>
  ...
</head>
```

Inline JavaScript should be used sparingly, if at all, as it has some downsides of its own: any script embedded directly in the page can't be cached as an individual file, so it will re-download with every new page that includes it. Further, inline scripts in the head of the page are downloaded in all browsers (and are executed in all JavaScript-capable browsers), which chips away at those precious first 14 kilobytes that make up our initial page rendering budget—jQuery alone typically weighs more than twice that, after all.

So what is inlining good for? It's good for the small, critical portion of your JavaScript codebase mentioned above (the shims, polyfills, etc.), but it should only be used for JavaScript that needs to be in the head.

But what if none of your JavaScript meets that criteria?

Loading from the bottom

A third approach to loading JavaScript is to place `script` elements at the end of an HTML document, allowing content to load and render as soon as possible, and forcing scripts to load and execute after the content itself has been parsed and rendered. A clear advantage to this method is that users can interact sooner with the page.

Alas, it too suffers from some notable limitations. First, this approach shares the same problem as `head`-referenced scripts in that there's no way to qualify a script's request or execution—it's fetched in all JavaScript-enabled browsers. Also, scripts referenced at the end of a document are *requested* much later, and take more time to load and execute than a script referenced higher in the page. This may be okay depending on whether or not your JavaScript affects the page presentation, but any visual enhancements JavaScript makes to the page can potentially cause a flash of un-enhanced content, so this is something to watch out for.

Back to the top with defer and async attributes

In modern browsers like IE10 (and pretty much every other browser for years now), the `async` and `defer` attributes can be added to `script` elements to instruct the browser to load a referenced JavaScript file in parallel while the HTML is still loading (`async`), and/or to execute the script after the HTML has finished loading (defer). These attributes can be used independently or together on a single script element.

```
<script src="myScript.js" async defer></script>
```

If there's no rush to execute a given script, the defer attribute can be great for page-loading performance, because it frees the browser to work on other essential tasks with a higher priority. Examples of scripting you might choose to defer include those that apply behavior to components that will be lazy-loaded themselves or that control content toward the end of a page, like blog comments.

That said, it's often preferable for JavaScript files to execute as soon as possible, so defer may not be ideal. For scripts that can safely execute as soon as they're ready, regardless of how much of the HTML document has loaded, the async attribute is best.

What's great about the async attribute is that it can be applied to script elements in the head (assuming they reference an external file), telling the browser to request a referenced file immediately, but to go ahead and begin rendering the page while that file loads in parallel—the best of both worlds.

```
<head>
  ...
  <script src="myScript.js" async></script>
  ...
</head>
```

And now the inevitable downsides. First, though support is fairly broad for these attributes, they won't stop scripts from blocking rendering in non-supporting browsers, like Android 2. IE9 and older lack async support but do support defer (in IE versions 5 and up), so you can combine the two with defer as a fallback.

Second, async doesn't guarantee that multiple scripts will execute in the order they're specified in the page source. While defer should guarantee execution order, it still fails to do so in IE9 and older. If you don't need to load multiple scripts that depend on one another, this won't be an issue.

Last, like all of the approaches above, the `async` and `defer` attributes offer no means of *qualifying* whether a script is requested or executed in the first place. To do so, we often need to rely on tools beyond those native to the browser in developing a responsible cross-device site.

A happy medium: loading scripts dynamically using a small inline script

Our final option for loading JavaScript is the one I recommend most. Dynamic loading allows us to decide based on any number of conditions whether or not to load additional files and, if so, request those files in a non-blocking manner. In a codebase designed to address a wide variety of network conditions, device features, and user preferences, dynamic loading is the most responsible approach we can take because it allows us to load only what's necessary and nothing more.

Loading JavaScript dynamically is straightforward: place a bit of JavaScript inline in the page and use that script to append additional `script` elements, which will download and execute in parallel. While there are several ways to dynamically append elements to a page with JavaScript, the `insertBefore` method is the safest and most reliable. Here's an example of how we can use `insertBefore` to load a script ("myScript.js") from the `head` of an HTML document:

```
<head>
  ...
  <script>
    var myJS = document.createElement( "script" );
    myScript.src = "myScript.js";
    var ref = document.getElementsByTagName( »
      "script" )[ 0 ];
    ref.parentNode.insertBefore( myJS, ref );
  </script>
</head>
```

Let's break down what's happening in this snippet:

- In the first two lines, we create a `script` element referenced by the variable `myJS`, and set its `src` to "myScript.js".
- In the next line, we create a variable `ref` to store a reference to the first `script` element found in the page (which could very well be the one that contains the script example above).
- Finally, we call the `insertBefore` method on the parent of `ref` (the `head` element in this case), specifying that `myJS`—which refers to the `script` element we're inserting—should be inserted just before `ref`.

After it runs, if you were to inspect the DOM you'd see this result (newly appended and loaded script in bold):

```
<head>
  . . .
  <script src="myScript.js"></script>
  <script>
    var myJS = document.createElement( "script" );
    myScript.src = "myScript.js";
    var ref = document.getElementsByTagName( »
      "script" )[ 0 ];
    ref.parentNode.insertBefore( myJS, ref );
  </script>
</head>
```

This pattern forms the foundation of many of the more fully featured asset-loading scripts in use today; indeed, I use it on almost every site I build. The big limitation to keep in mind is that if you need to load multiple script files that depend on one another, this approach can lead to trouble: it does nothing to ensure that scripts will execute in the order they are requested. That said, if you're combining all of your enhancement scripts into one file (I recommend doing that if you can keep its size reasonably small), this script alone may suit your needs just fine. I've packaged the script from this example into a reusable function called `loadJS` (http://bkaprt.com/rrd/4-35/). Here it is in action, with the text in bold telling `loadJS` to load the same script as in the examples above:

```
<script>
  /* Include the loadJS function */
  function loadJS( src ){ ... }
  loadJS( "myScript.js" );
</script>
```

With this handy tool at our disposal, we can have very little code in the `head` of our page and enhance the experience without blocking the page from loading quickly.

Enhancing responsibly

Imagine you need to develop a site that calls for fancy additions to the interface. These enhancements need more JavaScript and CSS than you can fit in the initial batch of code sent to all browsers. But you don't want to burden every browser with the additional code and requests—only the browsers that can use them.

Cutting the mustard

Just as we can qualify CSS rules with `@media only all`, we can broadly qualify the application of JavaScript enhancements as well. Sometimes, these broad qualifications align with features that are necessary for a website's enhanced experience, but they can also be used as a more general diagnostic for modern feature support.

In his article "Cutting the Mustard," BBC developer Tom Maslen describes approaching enhancements as a "two-tiered responsive solution" (http://bkaprt.com/rrd/4-36/). Depending on their capabilities, browsers receive either a functional, simple HTML-only experience or the enhanced version. To test whether a browser is up to snuff, the BBC came up with a diagnostic to see if a browser supports certain features—if it cuts the mustard, so to speak. If the browser passes, it gets the enhanced experience. In his article, Maslen mentions the following diagnostic as an example:

```
if( "querySelector" in document
  && "localStorage" in window
  && "addEventListener" in window ){
  // This browser cuts the mustard!
}
```

In this case, they've checked for the presence of three JavaScript methods that must be defined to proceed: `querySelector`, `localStorage`, and `addEventListener`, which will pass in a browser like IE9 but not in others like IE8. Now, the mustard in question may differ depending on the needs of each site. For example, the *Boston Globe* site uses media-query support as its gauge:

```
if( window.matchMedia && window.matchMedia( »
  "only all" ) ){
  // This browser cuts the mustard!
}
```

Testing qualifiers helps to ensure that we only apply enhanced scripting and styles in places that can understand them. (In addition, we can always introduce more specific feature tests to qualify the use of features that require more careful fallbacks.) Qualifying our enhancements makes QA testing easier too: when you know that a particular browser doesn't "cut the mustard," you can take comfort in the fact that people won't encounter usability issues, since you're leaving the experience as functional as it was in the first place.

Once my mustard is cut, I like to start the enhancement process by applying a class to the `html` element called `enhanced`:

```
document.documentElement.className += " enhanced";
```

I sometimes use `.enhanced` within CSS selectors applying styles that should only occur in qualified environments, as in this snippet that hides checkboxes inside labels in enhanced environments (assuming they'd be replaced by something like a custom check icon):

```
.enhanced label input[type=checkbox] {
  opacity: 0;
}
```

Now, qualifying the *application* of code is important, but qualifying whether or not additional code gets requested is important as well, since it's always best to avoid making superfluous HTTP requests. Let's move on to loading some assets in a qualified manner.

Qualified asset loading

If our aim is to load only one script file dynamically, the `loadJS()` pattern shown earlier is all we need, and we can qualify it with any conditions we'd like so that the file is only requested in browsers that are up to the task. For example, here's a snippet that will load our script in any `querySelector`-supporting browser (such as IE8 and newer):

```
// Check if browser supports querySelector
if( "querySelector" in document ){
  // This browser cuts the mustard!

  // first, let's add a class to the HTML element
  document.documentElement.className += " enhanced";

  // next, let's load our enhancement scripts
  loadJS( "myScript.js" );
}
```

Now we're getting somewhere! Let's tie this into our CSS-loading approach to get an idea of the bigger picture.

BRINGING IT ALL TOGETHER

We've covered loading our many assets in isolation, but loading them all efficiently in the same codebase requires organization and care. To finish this section off, let's walk through how our HTML, CSS, and JavaScript can be assembled to deliver quickly and responsibly.

The head of the page is the point from which we control the page enhancement process, so let's focus on that. Within the head, we will use techniques referenced throughout this section, like inlining both our critical CSS and the JavaScript that will help us load additional scripts, styles, and fonts in a qualified manner.

To help with this process, I've updated the Enhance project (which you may recall from earlier in the book) to host an example of the JavaScript workflow that we use for enhancing a page (FIG 4.26). A project file, enhance.js, contains the code from the loadCSS() and loadJS() functions mentioned earlier, as well as some helper functions for getting and setting cookies, fetching values from meta elements, and a sample *cut the mustard* to boot. Unlike a JavaScript framework, enhance.js is meant to be an editable boilerplate, so when you use it, delete whatever you don't need and add whatever makes sense for your project. The following examples use enhance.js for the inline JavaScript portion of our workflow.

That is so meta

First, we know we have a few files we may want to load with JavaScript; I like to start by defining those files' URLs in an easy-to-find place. Meta elements are great for that, so I'll place a few of those at the top of the head: one for our site's full CSS file, one for our custom fonts, and one for our JavaScript enhancements.

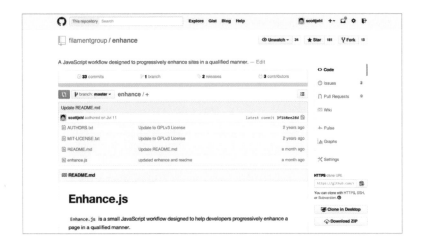

FIG 4.26: The Enhance project on Github (http://bkaprt.com/rrd/4-37/).

```
<head>
  ...
  <meta name="fullcss" content="/path/to/full.css">
  <meta name="fonts" content="/path/to/fonts.css">
  <meta name="fulljs" content="/path/to/ »
    enhancements.js">
  ...
</head>
```

Adding our critical JavaScript

With the `meta` tags in place, we can add our inline scripting. Again, this inline scripting should consist of only the JavaScript required to potentially enhance the experience. I typically include a modified version of `enhance.js` containing any functions and site-specific logic I may need. In this case, we want to be able to dynamically load our site's full CSS file without any qualification (since it contains styles that apply to all environments) and check to see if the browser passes the mustard test. If it does, we'll want to be able to load our custom fonts and enhanced JavaScript as well. (Note: you may choose to load custom fonts for everyone, but we typically reserve them for modern browsers, where they'll be most appreciated.)

Here's our updated head section with the inline script in place (additions in bold).

```
<head>
  ...
  <meta name="fullcss" content="/path/to/full.css">
  <meta name="fonts" content="/path/to/fonts.css">
  <meta name="fulljs" content="/path/to/ »
    enhancements.js">
  <script>
    {% include path/to/enhance.js %}
  </script>
  ...
</head>
```

Within that enhance.js file, alongside functions like loadC-SS() and loadJS(), is another function called getMeta(), which attempts to find a meta element by its name attribute. As a first step, we can find the meta element referencing our site's full CSS file with the following call:

```
getMeta( "fullcss" );
```

Once we have a reference to that meta element, we can get its content property to find the URL we need, and load the CSS file using loadCSS():

```
var cssMeta = getMeta( "fullcss" );
if( cssMeta ){
  // Load the site's full CSS file from the meta
  // element's content attribute
  loadCSS( cssMeta.content );
}
```

And that's all we need to do to load our site's full CSS file asynchronously.

Next within that inline script, we'll want to see if the browser passes our test before further enhancing the page by adding a class and loading our enhanced JavaScript and fonts. Here's how to do it:

```
...
// Check if browser supports querySelector
if( "querySelector" in document ){
  // This browser cuts the mustard!

  // First, let's add a class to the HTML element
  document.documentElement.className += " enhanced";

  // Next, let's load our enhancement scripting
  var jsMeta = getMeta( "fulljs" );
  if( jsMeta ){
  loadJS( jsMeta.content );
  }

// Finally, let's load our custom fonts
var fontsMeta = getMeta( "fonts" );
if( fontsMeta ){
  loadCSS( fontsMeta.content );
  }
}
```

That's it for the JavaScript.

Next in the head of the page, let's add the critical CSS necessary to render the top portion of the page. As a reminder, this critical CSS will vary from template to template, and should be generated by a tool like Grunt-CriticalCSS, which I mentioned in the CSS section earlier. We put that subset of CSS directly in the head, like so (additions in bold):

```
<head>
  ...
  <meta name="fullcss" content="/path/to/full.css">
  <meta name="fonts" content="/path/to/fonts.css">
```

```
<meta name="fulljs" content="/path/to/ »
  enhancements.js">
<style>
  /* Critical CSS styles for this template go
    here... */
</style>
<script>
  {% include path/to/enhance.js %}
</script>
...
</head>
```

Again, since the `script` and `style` elements reference no external code, their order in the page source won't affect rendering performance. That said, placing the critical CSS before the `script` ensures that the JavaScript will insert the full CSS file after the inline styles, so none of those will override the styles in the full CSS.

Next, I like to include a static reference to a site's full CSS file for browsers that don't have JavaScript enabled. That way we can make sure that all of the CSS will load regardless of whether or not we are able to load it dynamically using JavaScript. Here's that last addition in bold:

```
<head>
  ...
  <meta name="fullcss" content="/path/to/full.css">
  <meta name="fonts" content="/path/to/fonts.css">
  <meta name="fulljs" content="/path/to/ »
    enhancements.js">
  <script>
    {% include path/to/enhance.js %}
  </script>
  <style>
    /* Critical CSS styles for this template go
      here... */
  </style>
```

```
<noscript>
  <link rel="stylesheet" href="/path/to/full.css">
</noscript>
  . . .
</head>
```

Whew! And that's it. After that in the page source, the body element should follow containing all the functional HTML content required for that page to be useful to everyone.

Optimizing for subsequent loads using cookies

But there's a little more you can do. While the above workflow is fantastically optimized for the first time a user visits a site, we can take advantage of caching to make things load even faster on subsequent visits.

The main thing we can optimize is the inline CSS, which only needs to be present on the first visit before the site's full CSS has been requested and cached by the browser. After the initial visit, the browser will have already requested the full CSS and stored it in a local cache, so it's safe to reference that CSS from the head of the page in place of any inline CSS a template would otherwise include. Pulling this off requires adding a little server-side logic to your template, so your page will need to be running on a web server that has at least basic server-side scripting, like the ability to detect cookies. If you have access to that sort of environment, the setup for this optimization can be fairly straightforward.

First, you want to configure the head of your document to include its inline CSS or not based on the existence of a cookie, which we'll call fullcss for the sake of this example. Here's how the head will look with that check in place:

```
<head>
  . . .
  <meta name="fullcss" content="/path/to/full.css">
  <meta name="fulljs" content="/path/to/ »
    enhancements.js">
```

```
<script>
  {% include /path/to/enhance.js %}
</script>
{% if cookie "fullcss=true" %}
  <link rel="stylesheet" href="/path/to/full.css">
{% else %}
  <style>
    /* Critical CSS styles for this template go
    here... */
  </style>
  <noscript>
    <link rel="stylesheet" href="/path/to/full.css">
  </noscript>
{% endif %}
  ...
</head>
```

Next, within the inline JavaScript just after loading the site's full CSS file, you want to set a cookie to declare that the CSS file has been requested and cached. This cookie is stored in the browser and travels along with every subsequent request it makes to the server, which means it can be detected when serving subsequent pages and allow the logic above to detect it. Also, for subsequent page loads, the JavaScript should make sure that the cookie hasn't already been set before it loads the site's full CSS (since that CSS may already be included in the page).

Here's how that looks using enhance.js's cookie function (new code in bold):

```
var cssMeta = getMeta( "fullcss" );
if( cssMeta ){
  // Load the site's full CSS file from the meta
  // element's content attribute
  loadCSS( cssMeta.content );
  // set a cookie called "fullcss" to true
  cookie( "fullcss", "true" );
}
```

And that's *really* it!

If you'd like to see this example in action, check out the EnhanceJS site (http://bkaprt.com/rrd/4-37/), which has functional demo files matching the workflow shown here.

Go forth and load responsibly

By using the simple loading workflow above, we can carefully deliver assets only where they need to go and, best of all, serve pages that render incredibly fast for our users. The benefits of qualifying requests for large code enhancements cannot be overstated, as each request can add seconds to a user's page-load time (particularly on a mobile connection).

YOU GOT SERVED

We've covered a lot in this chapter, from optimizing our assets to discovering how to responsibly load them (or not!) in our pages for speedy rendering. Sites are more than just collections of pages; they're complex systems that can easily get weighed down if we aren't vigilant. Though this is still a period of transition, we appear to be on our way to lighter, brighter experiences. Let's contemplate what the future has in store.

CONCLUSION

Throughout this book, I've shared ways to build responsive sites that prioritize usability, access, sustainability, and performance. All of these factors matter for today's web, but they also ready our sites for the browsers of tomorrow.

Our audience is diversifying both geographically and technologically. As people in developing regions gain greater access to the web, the opportunity to broaden our reach grows as well, and the need for more fault tolerance and tiered, qualified delivery becomes ever more critical. At the same time, building responsibly benefits audiences in developed areas too, with faster, more accessible sites that are forgiving when browsing conditions are less than ideal. The contexts in which our users experience the web vary wildly, yet the demand for experiences that consider each person's browsing conditions, constraints, and expectations seems universal.

A responsible, responsive future

We can't predict what the future of the web holds, but we can prepare ourselves to embrace the unknowns ahead. To deliver on the promise of a widely accessible, delightful, and sustainable web experience, successful responsive designs must be integrated with other best practices. Embracing device and network diversity, and focusing on features and constraints rather than on browsers and devices, are our way forward.

The web was founded on the premise of broad access and inclusivity, and its unique, tiered application of technologies provides the scaffolding that lets us build upward without leaving anyone out. To meet that goal, we need to think creatively, build responsibly, and always keep our users at the forefront of our priorities.

May your reach be extended, your failures graceful, and your aims empathetic. Thanks so much for reading along.

ACKNOWLEDGEMENTS

I regret that in such a small space it's impossible for me to list all of the people whose talent and generosity made this book a reality. The best I can do is offer some highlights.

From early on, my family has been selflessly supportive of me: Mom, Dad, Kristen, Adam, my grandparents (thanks, Gram!). Thanks to my parents for sending me to learn design at Flagler College, where I met Randy Taylor, a talented designer and mentor who remains a good friend to this day. Randy, along with Seth Ferreira, encouraged me to integrate web design into my curriculum and introduced me to early clients like Dorothy Hesson at the Florida School for the Deaf & the Blind. Dorothy's passion and knowledge inspired my drive to build for access.

Thanks to Jon Reil, who took a chance and hired me fresh out of college. To Jeffrey Zeldman, Eric Meyer, and Jeremy Keith, each of whom I once considered distant heroes and am grateful to now consider friends. To Paul Irish, Steve Souders, Ilya Grigorik, and Andy Hume, who have shaped my understanding of web performance. To John Resig for welcoming me to the jQuery team early on. To the brilliant web community that I learn from every day: Jake Archibald, Tim Kadlec, Trent Walton, Dave Rupert, Chris Coyier, Mat Marquis, Bryan and Stephanie Rieger, Stephen Hay, Nicole Sullivan, Dan Cederholm, Brad Frost, Jason Grigsby, Josh Clark, Luke Wroblewski, Anna Debenham, James Craig, Karl Swedberg, and Lyza Gardner... the list goes on.

The highest of fives to my team at Filament Group: Patty Toland, Todd Parker, Maggie Wachs, Zach Leatherman, Jeff Lembeck, and John Bender. Each day I'm fortunate to work with some of the smartest, most caring people in this field. Nearly every line in this book is based on research that all of us produced or reviewed on company time. Patty and Todd run a special company that somehow manages to contribute an enormous amount of open-source projects, produce interesting and important work, and prioritize a generous life/work balance. I'm so grateful for them and what they've made for all of us.

I owe an enormous debt to A Book Apart and this editorial team. Tina Lee provided numerous rounds of restructuring, questions, and smart cuts, organizing my messy thoughts into a much clearer narrative. Mandy Brown, my first contact at ABA, provided critical directional editing. Katel LeDu, the managing director, was massively proficient in keeping our team on task and collaborating effectively. Rob Weychert's and Jason Santa Maria's talents transformed a column of text into the beautifully designed form you're now reading.

A special thanks to Ethan Marcotte. In addition to conceiving the practice on which this book is based, Ethan has long been a role model, not only for his well-known contributions to our field but also for the courteous manner in which he carries himself. Ethan was the tech editor and provided many rounds of code review, but he also offered important directional feedback and wasn't afraid to tell me when passages weren't hitting the mark. I'm deeply honored that Ethan wrote the foreword, and I'm very proud to call him my friend.

Last, but most important, thanks to my brilliant and talented wife Stephanie. This book was written on nights and weekends, during time that Steph and I would have otherwise spent together. Steph not only sacrificed sleep and leisure time (during a pregnancy, no less!) but also offered sage advice for many parts of this text. When the book was halfway written, our daughter, Emory, was born, and she will be a year old when it goes to print. Since books are Emory's favorite "toy," I like to think that one day she'll appreciate that her dad made one of those toys too. Steph and Emory deserve my greatest gratitude. I love you both.

RESOURCES

Devices, browsers, and testing

- **BrowserStack:** If you're building cross-device sites, you're going to need access to many devices. BrowserStack offers live testing in an expanding number of operating systems and browsers. Highly recommended (http://bkaprt.com/rrd/5-01/).
- **Can I use…:** A great resource for discovering how well features are covered across browsers today (http://bkaprt.com/rrd/5-02/).
- **Akamai's State of the Internet:** This report details connection speed and coverage trends for global internet access (http://bkaprt.com/rrd/5-03/).
- **StatCounter:** While certainly not comprehensive of all web traffic, StatCounter is recommended as a trusted source in browser and operating-system statistics worldwide (http://bkaprt.com/rrd/5-04/).
- **"Grade Components, Not Browsers":** This post argues for an evolved method of documenting differences in user experience across browsers (http://bkaprt.com/rrd/5-05/).

Performance optimization and analysis

- **WebPagetest:** A terrific service that analyzes how your site loads from various parts of the world in different browsers and devices (http://bkaprt.com/rrd/5-06/).
- **PageSpeed Insights:** A fast, browser-based service that helps you track areas to optimize site performance (http://bkaprt.com/rrd/5-07/).
- **Grunt-PerfBudget:** A command-line task from Tim Kadlec to automate performance testing with WebPagetest (http://bkaprt.com/rrd/5-08/).
- **"Setting a Performance Budget":** Tim Kadlec's post outlines the primary considerations that go into establishing site budgets (http://bkaprt.com/rrd/5-09/).

- **"Test on Real Mobile Devices without Breaking the Bank":** Brad Frost offers some excellent advice on building a well-balanced lab (http://bkaprt.com/rrd/5-10/).
- **Steve Souders:** Souders is the web performance guru. Keep up with his posts (http://bkaprt.com/rrd/5-11/)!
- **Building a Performance Culture:** This great talk by Lara Swanson and Paul Lewis covers the challenges and benefits of prioritizing performance within a company (http://bkaprt.com/rrd/5-12/).
- **Open Device Lab:** Find a device-testing lab in your area (http://bkaprt.com/rrd/5-13/).

Future-friendly coding practices and tools

- **Server-side feature detection:** The HTTP Client-Hints proposal from Ilya Grigorik of Google will enable browsers to send standardized information about their features and conditions to the server with each request they make. Keep an eye on the proposal's progress (http://bkaprt.com/rrd/5-14/).
- **CSS loading:** A number of potential solutions for loading inapplicable or low-priority CSS are being discussed in the www-style mailing list at the W3C (http://bkaprt.com/rrd/5-15/). So far, ideas like an onmatch attribute for link elements have been proposed (http://bkaprt.com/rrd/5-16/).
- **Feature testing:** Many features shouldn't be used without first checking that they're properly supported. Modernizr is the best feature-detection library currently available (http://bkaprt.com/rrd/5-17/).
- **Responsive images:** Opera's article "Responsive Images: Use Cases and Documented Code Snippets to Get You Started" is a must-read for those interested in using responsive images now (http://bkaprt.com/rrd/5-18/). Be sure to keep up with the RICG (http://bkaprt.com/rrd/5-19/) and Picturefill (http://bkaprt.com/rrd/5-20/) as well.
- **Filament's open-source projects:** Filament hosts a growing number of well-tested responsive components and tools you can use for free (http://bkaprt.com/rrd/5-21/).

- **Filament's SouthStreet:** This page hosts information and links to projects related to Filament's progressive enhancement workflow (http://bkaprt.com/rrd/5-22/).

REFERENCES

Shortened URLs are numbered sequentially; the related long
URLs are listed below for reference.

Introduction

0-01 http://www.wired.com/2014/01/internet-org-hackathon-low-end-rules/

0-02 http://www.moneyweb.co.za/moneyweb-south-africa-asia-mobile-internets-tomorrow

0-03 http://appleinsider.com/articles/12/02/17/apple_sold_more_ios_devices_in_2011_than_total_macs_in_28_years

0-04 http://www.cisco.com/c/en/us/solutions/collateral/service-provider/visual-networking-index-vni/white_paper_c11-520862.html

0-05 http://www.pewinternet.org/fact-sheets/mobile-technology-fact-sheet/

0-06 http://opensignal.com/reports/fragmentation-2013/

0-07 https://twitter.com/Cennydd/status/362269441645481984

0-08 http://alistapart.com/article/responsive-web-design

0-09 http://trentwalton.com/2014/03/10/device-agnostic/

0-10 https://www.flickr.com/photos/janitors/12907608763

0-11 https://www.flickr.com/photos/scottvanderchijs/5453911636

0-12 https://www.apple.com/accessibility/osx/voiceover/

0-13 http://www.google.com/think/research-studies/the-new-multi-screenworld-study.html

0-14 http://developer.android.com/about/dashboards/index.html

0-15 http://dev.opera.com

0-16 http://www.guypo.com/mobile/what-are-responsive-websites-made-of/

0-17 http://httparchive.org/interesting.php?a=All&l=Apr%2015%202014

0-18 http://minus.com/msM8y8nyh#1e

0-19 http://www.webperformancetoday.com/2013/03/19/new-findings-typical-leading-european-commerce-site-takes-7-04-seconds-to-load/

Chapter 1

1-01 http://trentwalton.com/2011/05/10/fit-to-scale/

1-02 http://the-pastry-box-project.net/dan-mall/2012-september-12/

1-03 https://twitter.com/brad_frost/status/191977076000161793

1-04 http://webtypography.net/2.1.2

1-05 http://webtypography.net

1-06 http://daverupert.com/2013/04/responsive-deliverables/

1-07 http://getbootstrap.com/

1-08 http://www.lukew.com/ff/entry.asp?1569

1-09 http://demos.jquerymobile.com/1.4.2/table-reflow/

1-10 http://demos.jquerymobile.com/1.4.2/table-column-toggle/

1-11 http://bradfrost.github.io/this-is-responsive/patterns.html

1-12 http://touchlab.mit.edu/publications/2003_009.pdf

1-13 http://www.smashingmagazine.com/2012/02/21/finger-friendly-design-ideal-mobile-touchscreen-target-sizes/

1-14 http://static.lukew.com/TouchGestureCards.pdf

1-15 https://github.com/filamentgroup/tappy

1-16 https://github.com/ftlabs/fastclick/

1-17 http://www.w3.org/WAI/intro/aria

1-18 http://www.nytimes.com/2013/12/30/opinion/america-in-2013-as-told-in-charts.html

1-19 http://filamentgroup.com/lab/grade_components/

1-20 http://adactio.com/journal/6692/

Chapter 2

2-01 http://alistapart.com/article/testing-websites-in-game-console-browsers

2-02 https://twitter.com/anna_debenham/status/246613439814971393

2-03 http://www.lukew.com/ff/entry.asp?1333

2-04 http://trentwalton.com/2013/03/19/type-touch/

2-05 https://www.flickr.com/photos/frankieroberto/2317229560/

2-06 http://www.slideshare.net/bryanrieger/rethinking-the-mobile-web-by-yiibu

2-07 http://blog.cloudfour.com/the-ems-have-it-proportional-media-queries-ftw/

2-08 http://trentwalton.com/2013/01/16/windows-phone-8-viewport-fix

2-09 http://caniuse.com

2-10 http://www.stucox.com/blog/the-good-and-bad-of-level-4-media-queries

2-11 http://alistapart.com/article/testdriven

2-12 http://modernizr.com/

2-13 http://dev.w3.org/csswg/css-conditional/#at-supports

2-14 http://dev.w3.org/csswg/css-conditional/#support-definition

2-15 https://github.com/Modernizr/Modernizr/wiki/Undetectables

2-16 http://filamentgroup.com/lab/overthrow

2-17 https://github.com/filamentgroup/fixed-fixed

2-18 https://github.com/aFarkas/html5shiv/#why-is-it-called-a-shiv

2-19 https://github.com/aFarkas/html5shiv

2-20 http://remysharp.com/2010/10/08/what-is-a-polyfill/

2-21 https://github.com/paulirish/matchMedia.js

2-22 https://github.com/scottjehl/Respond

2-23 http://adactio.com/journal/5964/

2-24 http://bradfrostweb.com/blog/mobile/test-on-real-mobile-devices-without-breaking-the-bank/

2-25 http://opendevicelab.com

2-26 https://www.flickr.com/photos/lukew/6171909286/

2-27 http://www.browserstack.com

Chapter 3

3-01 http://contentsmagazine.com/articles/10-timeframes/

3-02 http://httparchive.org

3-03 http://moto.oakley.com

3-04 http://www.stevesouders.com/blog/2011/09/21/making-a-mobile-connection/

3-05 http://devtoolsecrets.com

3-06 https://developers.google.com/speed/pagespeed/insights

3-07 http://webpagetest.org/

3-08 http://timkadlec.com/2014/01/fast-enough/#comment-1200946500

3-09 http://calendar.perfplanet.com/2013/holistic-performance

3-10 http://timkadlec.com/2014/05/performance-budgeting-with-grunt

3-11 http://imageoptim.com

3-12 http://optipng.sourceforge.net

3-13 http://jpegclub.org/jpegtran

3-14 https://github.com/gruntjs/grunt-contrib-imagemin

3-15 http://2012.dconstruct.org

3-16 http://www.gzip.org/deflate.html

3-17 http://html5boilerplate.com

3-18 https://developers.google.com/speed/docs/best-practices/caching

3-19 https://developer.mozilla.org/en-US/docs/Mozilla/Projects/Social_API/Service_worker_API_reference

3-20 http://www.html5rocks.com/en/tutorials/appcache/beginner

3-21 https://incident57.com/codekit/

3-22 http://gruntjs.com

Chapter 4

4-01 http://www.lukew.com/ff/entry.asp?933
4-02 http://24ways.org/2011/conditional-loading-for-responsive-designs
4-03 http://adactio.com/journal/5042/
4-04 https://github.com/filamentgroup/Ajax-Include-Pattern
4-05 http://filamentgroup.com/lab/ajax_includes_modular_content
4-06 https://github.com/filamentgroup/AppendAround
4-07 http://filamentgroup.github.io/AppendAround/
4-08 http://httparchive.org/interesting.php#renderStart
4-09 https://github.com/scottjehl/css-inapplicable-load
4-10 https://developers.google.com/speed/pagespeed/insights/
4-11 http://paul.kinlan.me/detecting-critical-above-the-fold-css/
4-12 https://github.com/filamentgroup/grunt-criticalcss/
4-13 https://github.com/filamentgroup/loadCSS
4-14 http://timkadlec.com/2012/04/media-query-asset-downloading-results/
4-15 http://boazsender.github.io/datauri
4-16 http://www.mobify.com/blog/data-uris-are-slow-on-mobile
4-17 http://filamentgroup.com/lab/rwd_img_compression
4-18 http://responsiveimages.org/
4-19 http://www.w3.org/TR/html-picture-element/
4-20 http://scottjehl.github.io/picturefill/
4-21 http://css-tricks.com/examples/IconFont/
4-22 http://filamentgroup.com/lab/bulletproof_icon_fonts
4-23 https://github.com/filamentgroup/a-font-garde
4-24 http://css-tricks.com/stackicons-icon-fonts
4-25 https://docs.google.com/presentation/d/1CNQLbqC0krocy_fZrM5fZ-YmQ2JgEADRh3qR6RbOOGk/edit?pli=1#slide=id.p
4-26 http://jakearchibald.com/2013/animated-line-drawing-svg/
4-27 http://css-tricks.com/svg-sprites-use-better-icon-fonts/
4-28 https://github.com/filamentgroup/grunticon
4-29 http://grumpicon.com
4-30 http://stet.editorially.com
4-31 http://dev.w3.org/csswg/css-font-loading
4-32 https://twitter.com/jaffathecake/status/207096228339658752
4-33 https://github.com/filamentgroup/shoestring
4-34 https://github.com/jquery/jquery#how-to-build-your-own-jquery

4-35   https://github.com/filamentgroup/loadJS
4-36   http://responsivenews.co.uk/post/18948466399/cutting-the-mustard
4-37   https://github.com/filamentgroup/enhance/

Resources

5-01   http://wwbrowserstack.com/
5-02   http://caniuse.com
5-03   http://www.akamai.com/stateoftheinternet
5-04   http://gs.statcounter.com/#all-browser_version_partially_combined-ww-monthly-201307-201407
5-05   http://filamentgroup.com/lab/grade-the-components.html
5-06   http://www.webpagetest.org
5-07   https://developers.google.com/speed/pagespeed/insights
5-08   http://timkadlec.com/2014/05/performance-budgeting-with-grunt
5-09   http://timkadlec.com/2013/01/setting-a-performance-budget
5-10   http://bradfrostweb.com/blog/mobile/test-on-real-mobile-devices-without-breaking-the-bank
5-11   http://stevesouders.com/
5-12   http://www1.practicalperformanceanalyst.com/2014/06/28/building-a-performance-culture-google-io-2014
5-13   http://opendevicelab.com
5-14   https://github.com/igrigorik/http-client-hints
5-15   http://lists.w3.org/Archives/Public/www-style
5-16   http://lists.w3.org/Archives/Public/www-style/2013Feb/0131.html
5-17   http://modernizr.com
5-18   http://dev.opera.com/articles/responsive-images
5-19   http://ricg.org
5-20   http://scottjehl.github.io/picturefill
5-21   http://filamentgroup.com/code
5-22   https://github.com/filamentgroup/Southstreet/

INDEX

U

Upstatement, 26
user agent detection, 70-71
user agent strings, 48-49

V

vector-based art, 140
viewport size detection, 51
viewport style settings, 60
Villamor, Craig, 28

W

W3C, 40, 60, 133
Wachs, Maggie, 44
Walmart, 12
Walton, Trent, 6, 15, 54, 60
web fonts, 151-54
WebPagetest, 97
Willis, Dan, 28
Wroblewski, Luke, 20, 28, 53, 109

X

x-ray perspective, 34

ABOUT A BOOK APART

We cover the emerging and essential topics in web design and development with style, clarity, and above all, brevity—because working designer-developers can't afford to waste time.

COLOPHON

The text is set in FF Yoga and its companion, FF Yoga Sans, both by Xavier Dupré. Headlines and cover are set in Titling Gothic by David Berlow.

MIX
Paper from responsible sources
FSC® C103203

This book was printed in the United States using FSC certified Finch papers.